Slipped Away

A MEMOIR

In Loving Memory of
Steve Tarpinian
December 1960 – March 2015

Jean Mellano

"...those of us who did make it have an obligation to build again, to teach to others what we know, and to try with what's left of our lives to find goodness and a meaning to this life."
- Charlie Sheen as Chris Taylor; Platoon [Motion picture]. (1986). Helmdale Film Corp.

Printed in the United States of America
ISBN: 978-0-692-53981-1
LCCN: 2015918111

ACKNOWLEDGEMENTS

This memoir had its origins in my social media tribute to Steve. For about a month after Steve passed away, on a daily basis, I would post a little story with photos about Steve, or about Steve and I. I am not much of a social media person, let alone broadcasting snippets of my life, but the overwhelming support I received from my online friends inspired me. My postings metamorphosized into a Photo Book. My next undertaking was to publish Steve's short story (Chapter 5), *A Mouse in the House*, as a children's book. I then began to feel very strongly, as did others, that Steve's story should be told, at which point I began writing my manuscript for a memoir of Steve.

I want to thank my very close friends, Judy Meier-Smollon, Mike Stewart Sr., Kathy Kerner and my cousin, Terry Connell. They have been by my side at every step through my journey of grief, offering me unconditional love and support. They put up with my tears and ranting and raving and I will forever be indebted to them.

Many thanks to my good friend Natalie Penny, Steve's head swim coach and Michael Stewart, Jr., a young triathlete Steve had mentored for providing me with beautiful tributes and their perspectives about Steve. Their writings are in Chapters 2 and 3 of the memoir.

The support of the triathlon community has been overwhelming. Some of the top names in the sport have told me they were honored to provide a contribution to the book, whether it was a quote or the Foreword. I was aware that Steve knew many people in the sport, but I had no idea how much respect people had for him. The sad thing is that I don't think Steve ever realized how much he was loved. Special thanks to Rip Esselstyn, Joe Friel, John Howard, Michael Lovato, Mike Plant, Whit Raymond, Dave Scott, Scott Tinley, Greg Welch, and the XTERRA organization —especially Tom Kiely and Janet Clark— for their support of this memoir.

My thanks also goes to Damaris Curran Herlihy for helping me make this book the best it can be and thanks also goes to Nick Sachs who has patiently worked with me on the printing and distribution of this book.

Last but not least, I want to thank the book's illustrator, Steve Dansereau. Steve is a man who, as Steve Tarpinian might describe, is facing his fears, living his dreams and pursuing his passion; art. He was so touched by this memoir and could have been a kindred spirit of Steve's. This book would not have come to fruition without him. He has been my advocate, my adviser and has provided such kind and gentle guidance. Steve has gotten me through times where I was going to give up on completing this project. I feel as though he is a partner with me on this book and I think Steve Tarpinian would approve.

FOREWORD

Dear Steve,

I still remember the first time we met at a USA Triathlon coaches meeting in Colorado Springs back in the 1990s. I noticed you then because you were a breath of fresh air in a room full of overly serious coaches. It soon became apparent to me that you didn't have any cards up your sleeve. There was no hidden agenda—then or ever. You were one of the most honest and open people I've ever known. I am a better person for having known you, Steve. I miss you.

Your friendly, but businesslike attitude, combined with your years of triathlon experience and knowledge made you a great teacher. But you were more than someone who just taught us how to swim, bike, and run. Much more importantly, you taught us how to be a good person. That was done through example rather than with words. I still remember your most important lessons as you treated everyone the same—unknown novice triathletes and seasoned pros. You made us all feel important. I miss that.

The last time our paths crossed was in Kona at the Ironman a few years ago. That's where I would usually see you every year. I looked forward to it. You were always happy and cheerful. Our friendship and conversations would start refreshed. Time marched on but we stayed on pace. We'd share new ways of training our athletes and talk about camps we were doing and how the world was treating us. We laughed about silly stuff, like how to steer a car with your knees while using both hands to eat a sandwich. I'll never forget you demonstrating how to make a U turn using only your knees. Other times we debated "serious" technical triathlon stuff such as where power was best measured, close to the tire-ground contact point or where the foot connects to the pedal. You know, important stuff like that. Those discussions made us better coaches and closer friends. I miss them.

We all trusted and looked up to you because of how you made us feel about ourselves. Your cheerful demeanor and smile were infectious. It was always apparent to me that athletes and coaches loved being around you, as I did. You were—and still are—held in high regard by all of us. It was always apparent that your primary interest was the athlete and not building your own reputation. You were a role model for many coaches, including me. I will miss that.

I will walk the streets of Kona again. I will be reminded of our friendship again. I will miss you, again!

Your friend,

Joe Friel

Contents

Slipped Away

INTRODUCTION

This memoir is dedicated to those who suffer from mental illness and their families. Mental illness is a very real disease. Many people are afraid to acknowledge it because it is so hard to understand what people with it are experiencing. It can strike at any age and may be debilitating. Families often feel devastated and powerless to help their loved ones who suffer from these illnesses. Unfortunately, like most people who live with mental illness, I have many questions about what I could have done differently; sadly, I have no answers. Not a day goes by after Steve's death that I don't say to myself, "I should have ...." or "What if I had said..." But I now realize there is nothing I could have done differently. Mental illness can be like a cancer of the mind. In Steve's case, it finally took over his mind and metastasized to his soul.

This book was a labor of love for me and has helped me work through my grief over the loss of the love of my life. I had to question myself as to what my goals were by publishing such a personal and private part of my life. I want to inspire conversation to help remove the stigma associated with mental illness. How often do we see in the headlines the story of a crime committed by an alleged perpetrator that has a history of mental illness? In his or her own way, the alleged perpetrator is a victim as well—a victim of a terrible disease that is capable of altering the mind to do something very out of character. Of course, not all crimes are committed by people with mental illness, just as all people with mental illness do not commit crimes. But mental illness is a disease that knows no bounds. Mental illness is nothing to be ashamed of, nor should it be swept under the rug. It's important to know that many individuals suffering from mental illness are not necessarily defined by the disease. Their lives can be productive and filled with joy, laughter, and love.

I want Steve's legacy to be his kind and compassionate self in spite of his own personal struggles. He was someone who impacted so many lives in a powerful and positive way. He gave so much to so many with no expectation of a return. Steve was not just a coach of sport, he was a coach of life and I learned so much from him. He was a gift to all of us and that gift was only ours to borrow.

The majority of the profits for the sale of this book will be donated to Project9line, a non-profit organization on Long Island (www.Project9line.org). You may wonder how I chose this organization. Throughout this entire process of publishing this book, I have felt the hand of Steve guiding me. I believe, as he did, there are no coincidences. One day, I dropped off some promotional bookmarks for the memoir at my chiropractor's office. I was directed to place them on a counter next to another stack of promotional cards that caught my eye. It was for Vet Stock, an event presented by Project9line to honor all veterans. I wanted to find out more about this organization as Steve and I both sympathized with the plight of our country's returning veterans. Project9line has a unique approach to assist returning veterans who may be suffering from PTSD and depression; they create multiple venues for the veterans to showcase their talent and share their experience through the arts.

What is the significance of Project9line? "9line" is derived from a very important U.S. Military protocol known as "9 line MEDEVAC." It is a procedure used on the battlefield when placing a call for assistance related to a casualty. A soldier must provide the nine most important facts about the scenario so the most effective help can be sent. I am sure Steve would want important facts of his own story to be told in an effort to help others with mental illness, just as Project9line is helping veterans when they return home.

Many years ago, Steve asked me if my corporate job was fulfilling and if I felt I was helping people with my career choice. I didn't understand why he was asking me this question since I chose my job based on my skills and the fact I needed to make a living. Now, in retrospect, I realize that with the career path choices Steve pursued, it was his mission in life to help people and he wanted to know if I shared that sentiment. He was a Jones Beach lifeguard, went through the process of applying to the New York City Fire Department, and finally became a coach to help people be the best they could be—both in life and in sport. Now, after so many years, I finally understand Steve's question and I hope by writing this book, it will serve to help people in some way. Perhaps the book proceeds can help develop a program that helps a returning veteran get through his or her depression or help an individual know they are not alone in dealing with mental illness and suicide. It is my sincerest hope that something good can come out of the tragic circumstances surrounding Steve's life.

Chapter One

Through
My
Eyes

CHAPTER ONE

These were most likely the final written words by my soul mate and love of my life for almost thirty-four years. They were found on a piece of paper in his wallet.

Reasons To Go

On March 15, 2015, Steve Tarpinian lost his war with depression. I use the term depression, but in reality his troubles were far more complex. Over the years, he was diagnosed with many mental illness labels: manic depressive, bipolar, personality disorder, obsessive compulsive with his thoughts, anxiety disorder, and so on. Whatever was troubling his mind manifested itself as a depressed state to those who knew him intimately—a state in which he could not function and would just want to stay in bed all day. Steve lost interest in the things he always seemed so passionate about. In his final few months, Steve frequently became so indecisive that he could no longer effectively live his life. Steve finally made the irreversible decision to leave behind his pain. On his second attempt to end his life, he succeeded.

Steve had won many battles in his private war. He appeared to most as a very happy, trouble-free person who had it all figured out. Steve had a very successful business, was a great athlete and a great coach, and he was loved by so many. He was very good at hiding his inner turmoil. Even as I read Steve's journals from over ten years ago, his writings indicate he was struggling with the same issues then that plagued him just weeks before his death. His mind was consumed by indecisiveness, obsessiveness, and regrets about not following certain paths in his life. Hindsight is twenty-twenty; I had no idea Steve's mind was so tortured for so many years, or perhaps I chose to close my eyes to it since I was so much in love with him.

In his confusing ramblings written to a family member earlier in January of 2015, Steve even questioned our relationship. In one sentence he wrote, "If I leave [Jean] it is like a death, if I stay [with Jean] it is another type of death." Yet he never shared those thoughts with me. Steve's communications with me always indicated how much he loved me and wanted to be with me always and forever. In February of 2015, he wrote in a journal, " I love Jean more than my life and can't imagine life without her." Did Steve take his life because he didn't want to hurt me by saying he wanted to leave me? Or, did he take his life because it was less painful to do that than face working on our relationship? Or, was his mind so ravaged by the mental illness, he could no longer think clearly? Sadly, I will never know.

One of his friends often said, "Oh, to have a day in the life of Steve Tarpinian." Little did that friend know that a day in the life of Steve Tarpinian, especially towards the end, was filled with pain.

Steve's final weeks were spent at an inpatient facility in Arizona. As with many things in his life, he struggled with making the decision to actually seek the help he so desperately needed. In several of his notes and writings that I have found since his death, more than once he expressed the following about admitting himself to this facility.

Reasons to go:

Get off of medications, especially Ativan.
Learn how to make decisions.
Learn how to handle regrets.
Learn how to handle change.
Live a happy life.

With the encouragement of those closest to him, he decided to check himself in. We spoke daily by phone and, for the most part, he seemed to be doing okay. We did not talk about work and kept the conversations light hearted. After almost a month, Steve told me he wanted to come home. I told him he could do that only if he felt strong enough to deal with his life back home—including his company and all its immediate issues. Steve lamented that he was not actively managing his company or providing proper fiduciary oversight, including the sale of all or parts of his business. In his depressed state, he was not capable of overseeing his business in any way. He was between a rock and a hard place. Steve had spent over twenty years building his business, profiting each year and never having taken out a loan. Now his business was in a downward spiral. He had already begun to use retirement money just to keep the company afloat.

I did my best to manage the business on Steve's behalf. I was so buried in the day-to-day details and minutiae of Steve's business and illness, I really could never grasp the big picture of what was happening. After Steve had passed, a good friend to Steve and me helped me take a step back so that I could open my eyes and see the forest through the trees. The business was failing and had been for quite some time.

Unsustainable

Steve's inability to run his company due to his depression was a major factor in its slow demise; however, there were other factors (some within his control and some not) that impacted his business that he could not or did not want to address.

The pace at which Steve's company was growing was unsustainable—a pace even a mentally healthy person would struggle to maintain. Steve worked seven days a week, sometimes leaving at 6 a.m. and not returning home until 10 p.m. By 2010, the membership of the triathlon team that he coached was close to 300 athletes. His event company was producing eleven adult and four youth multi-sport events annually in the span of seven months. This is in addition to having published three books, three swimming videos, and one yoga video. Add to that, Steve conducted annual multiple-day training camps in Montauk, Hawaii, Germany, Spain, and Lake Placid. The triathlon sport was exploding and Steve's company helped fuel that on Long Island.

He began to see more start-up event companies, more triathlon teams, and more coaches—creating a much more competitive environment for Steve's company. Athletes were expecting more amenities and lower registration fees, even as costs rose. Municipalities were making it more difficult to obtain permits for the events and their fees for these permits were sky-rocketing. Along the way, Steve continued pursuing his own athletic goals—training to complete an Ironman distance race every year (2.4 mile swim, 112 mile bike, and a 26.2 mile run), plus several other key races. All these factors together took their collective toll on Steve. Being clinically depressed and driving himself at a frenetic pace, Steve eventually became physically, emotionally, and mentally exhausted—he ended up paying the ultimate price.

In 2010, I retired from my career in information technology. With Steve's blessing, I brought structure, process, and policy to his fast-growing company. Over time, however, my corporate sensibilities clashed with Steve's business culture. I felt there were aspects of his business operation that would benefit from more professionalism and a more traditional corporate approach. I brought my concerns to his attention, but only met with resistance, causing a great deal of conflict between us. My greatest concern was Steve's desire to be friends with his employees. If there were issues with the business or with specific employees, he did not bring those issues to their attention for fear it would negatively impact their friendship and/or the employee might leave. Likewise, he feared hurting our relationship by not taking my advice, even if he felt it was the right thing to do.

Steve wrestled with his roles as a soul mate, friend, and business owner and manager. His way of handling this conflict and reducing my stress was to extract me from dealing with anything related to his company. How ironic that since I was the beneficiary of his estate, I was left to deal with the liabilities and obligations of his company—all while I was in a state of shock over his death and working through my own grief. The responsibility of managing his failing business is something Steve never would have wanted to leave for me. I managed to stabilize the company, then sold it to friends of Steve's who believe in his vision and will continue his triathlon legacy on Long Island.

While still at the Arizona facility, about a week to ten days before he passed, Steve said to me, "I am so afraid." When I asked what he meant, he could not—or did not want to—explain what he feared. Little did I know, he probably realized he was literally "losing his mind" and had no control over it. He felt he had no options left. This was my Ironman, my rock of support who got me through cancer and the passing of my parents—how could he possibly feel so vulnerable?

A psychiatrist explained to me that what Steve experienced was extremely tortuous to his mind. It was amazing he was able to accomplish all that he did. This is a true testament to the strength of the amazing human being that was Steve Tarpinian. He struggled many years with depression and tried so hard to fight this demon. During my life with him, for periods of time, Steve would seem to be okay and appear to be "cured." But with all of his own research, working closely with psychologists and psychiatrists, and getting help from emergency rooms, inpatient, and outpatient facilities toward the end of his life, the demon didn't stay away for long. During the early years of our relationship, the depressive episodes would happen maybe once a year and last for a few days. As time went on, the episodes would occur more frequently and last longer in duration. He had professionals treating him, medications helping him, and the love of his family, friends, and me. But there was nothing that could help him. In the end, his demon got the best of him.

The Abyss

Steve started slipping away from us in early 2013. Subconsciously, I believe this is when I started to mourn his loss. Steve started alternating through cycles of depression and clarity much more frequently. I was stuck in an abyss of hope, thinking that each time he would recover from a depressive episode, that this was the time he finally conquered this illness. Several times throughout 2013, Steve was in and out of inpatient and outpatient facilities. But nothing seemed to help him long term. Steve said he could not relate to the other patients in these hospitals and felt the doctors were just pumping him with more medications. Treatment was no longer effective for him.

Two vivid memories will be frozen forever in my mind. In the summer of 2013, I called 911 because Steve thought he was having a heart attack. I had three county EMS workers in my bedroom at 4:00 a.m. administering oxygen to Steve. After the ambulance ride to the emergency room, the examining doctor ruled out a heart attack and felt that Steve was having a panic attack. Within hours, Steve seemed to return to his old self again and he signed himself out of the hospital. Later that week, Steve had another panic attack. I drove him to an inpatient facility to be re-admitted (he was there for a few days earlier in the year). Steve was adamant he did not want to return and tried to get out of the car at a red light while we sat in the left-hand turning lane; to keep him in the car, I had to go through the light to prevent him from getting out in the middle of dangerous, fast-moving traffic. When we arrived at the facility, I got out of the car, sobbing, in search of someone who might admit him. I finally found a doctor and pleaded with him to help Steve. Steve walked up to the doctor and said he was fine and didn't need any help. Since these facilities require the patient to self admit, there was nothing the doctor could do. I thought perhaps it was I who was losing my mind. With the exception of his inner circle of family and very close friends, Steve had the ability to hide his inner turmoil very effectively from those around him.

For the end of 2013 and much of 2014, our life together was a rollercoaster of emotions. I was doing my best to survive in the midst of chaos. I was attempting to keep Steve's business running and our home in tact, while he was spiraling farther and farther into the depths of despair. More than once, Steve left a plate or pot on the lit stove unattended and set off the smoke detector. He was not only becoming a danger to himself, but to me and our home as well. A therapist told me I was experiencing "ambiguous loss"—when a loss occurs in our lives, but there is something making us feel stuck or unable to move forward in the grieving process. It can occur when a loved one may be physically present but psychologically absent. The normal grief process of denial, anger, bargaining, depression, and acceptance happened continually with me as I struggled to deal with Steve's rapid cycles of depression.

Despite his demon of depression, Steve accomplished much in his life. He was a visionary and an entrepreneur who built a successful multisport event and coaching company. He created videos/DVDs and books related to swimming and triathlons while pursuing his own athletic accomplishments, including completing eighteen Ironman Triathlons. However, Steve's true legacy is a kind, compassionate, and caring human being. He made a significant impact on so many people's lives. He did not let his mental illness define him. The primary purpose of writing this memoir is to share little snippets of the life of Steve Tarpinian as a way to demonstrate his great humanity and a life full of joy, love, and laughter.

A Lifetime of Love

Steve and I met on August 29, 1981, while I was roller-skating with some friends at Jones Beach. He was on a run with two fellow lifeguards. I don't know what came over me, but as the men ran passed, I skated after them and started whooping and hollering. Steve turned back to see what the commotion was and our eyes locked. In my excitement, I fell and Steve came back to help me up. I skated with the lifeguards as they ran for a little bit, then Steve asked if I wanted to come to a lifeguard party later that day. From then on, we were forever soul mates.

We lived ten life times in one. We experienced so many wonderful things together. Even after thirty-three plus years together, everything was a great adventure for us; whether it was travelling to beautiful places or just taking a walk in our neighborhood. After he passed, the pain was so intense that I truly felt myself wishing we had never fallen in love. I was very angry that he left me alone and also left me responsible for picking up the pieces of his life. However, I have clarity now. My pain and anger pale in comparison to the mental anguish Steve experienced on a day-to-day basis, especially towards the end.

As I created this memoir, I realized that Steve and I had something very special together that many people never have the opportunity to experience. Now my cherished memories of our time together make me realize that I am glad we shared a great love story, even though he is no longer here with me.

As with any relationship, Steve and I had some tough times, especially in the last few years—many of them related to his depression. However, we always seemed to bounce back and our love for each other continued to grow stronger. Even in the final moments of his life, he reached out to me with love. These were his final words to me in a text he sent within twenty minutes before he passed:

Sun, Mar 15, 11:42 AM

I love you more.

Steve touched the lives of so many and had so much to give in his short lifetime. My attempt in this book is to capture the essence of his love. In chapter two, you'll read about Natalie Penny, Steve's head swim coach who has been a tremendous support to both me and Steve over the past few years; she continues to be a huge support to me. In chapter three, you'll read a thesis written by a young triathlete Steve had mentored and coached that shows the tremendous positive influence Steve had on this young person's life. Chapter four provides the perspectives of many in the triathlon community, from beginners to current and past professionals. I do not know many of these people, but what they have said touched my soul and made me realize even more how special Steve was to so many. Chapter five contains some of Steve's writings: several poems, excerpts from his published and unpublished works, and a short story. I believe his short story captures the spirit of Steve's kind soul and how he would most likely want to be remembered. The final chapter has some of my favorite photos and stories demonstrating the wonderful and compassionate Steve Tarpinian.

Chapter Two

Through the Eyes of a Coach

CHAPTER TWO

"Steve wanted to be understood;
he wanted to understand himself."
—Natalie Penny

Natalie and her husband Nick first met Steve in April, 1996, at one of Steve's four-hour swim clinics on Long Island. Natalie thought to herself, "Four hours? I can barely swim for twenty minutes!" Natalie said this was the start of her own path of improvement with Steve as her guide.

Steve and Natalie met again in 2004. Nick found out that Steve had a training-group meeting weekly at the county aquatic center. Within a year, Natalie was training and working with Steve and a small youth group that was training together with adults as a family. With each year that passed, Natalie took on additional working and training roles until she was immersed in Steve Tarpinian's world—attending training camps, clinics, and seminars from Montauk to Lake Placid to Massachusetts, from Colorado to Mallorca, Spain; traveling to events as both an employee and athlete across Long Island, New York State, Germany, and the UK, and preparing others to do the same.

Below are Natalie's words on her perspective of Steve's depression and his slipping away.

Depressive states are unique to each individual and need to be addressed holistically. Steve's approach in helping others was, I would like to say, "always," (but Steve would correct me to say, "mostly") holistic. His coaching, educational and event services had to be of holistic benefit to those with whom he connected but in a state of reciprocity —reciprocity in goodwill and kindness. Steve had a holistic view of tremendous breadth and depth, which in the end was harmful to him. His connectedness to so many reached a tipping point where he became unable to manage his relationships with others. Steve mostly hid his current troubles from me, and preferred to carry on as if all was well and good in the final two years of his life. I saw him less and less and heard from him only sporadically. It was in Steve's silence that I knew things were deteriorating for him. In the calls we did have, he suffered memory loss and felt frustrated, but continued the conversation without addressing his current situation. December 2012 marked an almost complete end to his time on the pool deck coaching his team. As I walked off the deck, I listened to Steve ask that if we are present in the moment and things should be okay, what if they are never okay now? I noticed his lips were gray, his breath was off, and mouth dry. I just assumed he was having difficulty managing some work issues and that he would work through it, take a break and bounce back. Steve was invincible... Super strong... Super handsome... Super fit. He certainly had some days of clarity in 2013, but they became fewer and further between.

On the eve of the Montauk Lighthouse Sprint triathlon in 2009, we shared and compared childhood experience; Steve opened up to a darkness which had existed in his life since a time he was unable to pinpoint. At the time I dismissed it as not serious. Five to ten years ago, I thought Steve's lifestyle was fantastic, so different to that of anyone I knew, and I loved the person he chose to be now. More recently I recognized his pain and suffering and did all I could do to show support and friendship in the hope he would heal. Steve asked if I would love the dark side as well. I thought it was an odd question and wondered for a moment what he meant, but moved the subject on without answer—I'm thinking he took that as, no. Honestly, I never asked too many questions about Steve's dark side. I have come to accept that light and dark, just as good and bad, are not opposites, but rather co-exist, and in terms of our own relationship, I focused on the bright side and we enjoyed laughing at Austin Powers, Monty Python and the lighter side of dark themes.

Steve felt it both important and necessary to write things down. I found it interesting that while I, and most of us, primarily knew Steve through his coaching and event services, Steve thought of himself primarily as a writer, and as a trusted friend he shared several writing projects with me; he gave me the opportunity to co-write the swim portion of the USAT Junior Coaching Certification Program, as well as the Great Neck Public School Triathlon summer program. Steve shared many of his own published books, articles and presentations with me. He found his life's journey fascinating and was proud of the reach *he had both near and far in helping people to feel good, to feel better and be their own best. Steve was proud of his swimming background and choices to help people feel better and best with this in particular. He was very proud of the essay he wrote to be considered as a student athlete swimmer at Chaminade High School. Steve told me he was raised a Catholic but while he wasn't particularly religious, he was very spiritual and we shared, read and enjoyed the Eckhart Tolle books on being present in the here and now. One of his earliest writings stuck with me in terms of trying to figure out why Steve succumbed and slipped away into his own darkness. He showed and gave me his copy of a story he had written about Krikor Hekimian Tarpinian, his paternal grandmother's brother whom was believed to have perished in the Armenian Genocide Marches 100 years ago. This story was an early piece of writing which he had kept as a cherished piece and I felt honored that he trusted me to take it away, read it in my own time and return it. My own personal belief is to trace back the root cause of his particular depressive disorder to this time in history.*

Steve wanted to be understood; he wanted to understand himself.

As I sit and contemplate why Steve could no longer continue with himself, I understood the pattern of unraveling of relationships and the sting he felt in lack of reciprocity in caring of those around him. In some cases, this did happen, in others, they were perceived as such. Steve cared deeply for humanity and wondered when we would unite as one people. At one time, as we discussed it at length in a bakery in Syosset, he was hopeful it was coming soon. We did not agree on that. He felt a deep sadness at the cannibalistic tendencies of human nature. We often discussed being vegetarian, but what we were really talking about was the nature of those with whom we work and others with whom we compete. He perceived behaviors within his coaching and event teams as cannibalistic and threatening to his own existence. His lack of faith and trust in people became paralyzing. It is said that we cannot control the words or actions of others but we can control our own reaction to them. Steve lost the ability to control his reactions which were to withdraw and isolate himself. His isolation led to his disconnection from the people and activities he enjoyed; for a short while in the summer months of 2013 he had clarity in communication and seemed to be healing and heading in a positive direction. He expressed deep gratitude to those who stood by him; he wrote and spoke of his thanks often.

In the final months of Steve's life, he made efforts to return to the pool deck to coach sessions he had at one time never missed. Steve made a point of telling me he enjoyed himself and that he enjoyed coaching me and us that night or morning. Sessions which had burned him out and sapped his energy were beginning to give energy back to him and give him a sense of life worth living. We held on in the hope he would return; he let go. The energy was not enough to pull him through.

In his life, Steve recognized the impermanence of things—pain, sorrow, failure, success, fortune, and happiness. I am deeply saddened by the loss of Steve but feel he lived a tremendously full life and his path was the way it was supposed to be.

Steve and Natalie at the 2009 Montauk
Lighthouse Sprint Triathlon.

Chapter Three

Through the Eyes of a Student

CHAPTER THREE

*"Everything he did, and still does to this
day, is all in an effort to brighten
other people's days..."*
—Michael Stewart

This chapter is devoted to a short college thesis written by Michael Stewart, a junior triathlete Steve had coached and mentored. What makes it so poignant is that it was written in 2012 while Steve was still alive. Steve treasured these words and was so humbled by them. Steve had saved many notes and letters of gratitude from people whose lives he had touched over the years and I have found them in the strangest places in our house. I always knew Steve was a special soul, but seeing Michael's thesis and other notes and letters written to Steve truly affirm it.

I believe one of the things that helped Steve to carry on his battles against depression over the years was writings like Michael's. Otherwise, I think we would have lost him sooner. It seemed like Steve was in constant turmoil for most of his adult life, the depth of which was unbeknownst to those who loved him.

Michael taught me a very valuable lesson. It is so important to acknowledge people for what they have done for us while they are still alive and can truly appreciate the gratitude.

"Stewie" and Steve, 2010.

Michael Stewart's Thesis

Many individuals have greatly impacted my life. None, however, have come close to having as much influence on my life as Steve Tarpinian has. Recently, Steve and I have had little communication; yet, I want to take this time out to make sure Steve receives the full appreciation I never was able to show him. To this day, I consider Steve a second father to me. Because of how close we became, Steve Tarpinian's wisdom, generosity, and kindness positively influenced my life more than any other individual, giving me a true role model to look up to.

The first time I met Steve was at one of my father's triathlon competitions in Montauk, when I was only a couple of years old. My father had known Steve since before I was even born. Steve was the founder of Team Total Training, a triathlon team my father and I are members of. Steve also lived around the block from us. Steve's massive upper body combined with his six-foot figure and raging mullet made him quite an intimidating figure for any young child upon first glance. His beaming smile, however, gave Steve the appearance of a friendly giant, always offering positive vibes and encouragement to people, regardless of their ability. After only a minute of hearing Steve talk, people could realize that he is one of the nicest, most humble human beings to walk this earth.

Steve and I started to become close when I began attending some of my father's swim practices, when I was around eight or nine years old. As a child, I followed my father everywhere, aspiring, one day, to be just like him. As time progressed, my urge to swim with the team grew stronger and stronger. I wanted to try to fit in with all the adults. Finally, with my persistent urging, my father convinced Steve to stay after practice one day to take a look at my swim stroke. To this day, I'll never forget the first bit of coaching advice I ever received from Steve, which was to scrape my thumb against my thigh on my follow through to ensure I was finishing my stroke. Shortly after, I began swimming with some of the beginner adult swimmers at the practices. Steve not once questioned my father for dragging his then pre-teen son into swim practices with people at least three to four times my age. It was at this time I truly began to fall in love with the sport of triathlon.

Steve and I really started to bond after he created the Team Total Training junior division, which was one of the first training opportunities for children fourteen and younger who wanted to compete in triathlons. The first brochure for the junior team featured me and two other boys posing for the camera, after placing first, second, and third in the youngest age division at the Mighty North Fork Triathlon, held in Southold, New York. As my love and commitment for triathlons grew, so did my relationship with Steve. Not only was Steve my coach, he was one of my best friends, a second father to me. I looked up to Steve, as I still do, more than anyone else in the world. Steve would drive me to any Team Total Training practice I wanted to go to, and it was on these rides that our relationship flourished. I talked to Steve about everything; school, girls, work, etc. Often times, I valued Steve's opinion more than my own father's. From the ages thirteen to sixteen, I did everything in my power to be just like Steve. He was a role model in every sense of the term. Whether it was driving me to practices, paying for my meals when we would go out to eat, or helping out a friend in need, there was never a time I saw Steve make a selfish decision. Simply put, Steve loved making people feel good about themselves. Everything he did, and still does to this day, is all in an effort to brighten other people's days, which is what inspired me to be just like Steve.

Unfortunately, as the latter years of high school wore on, I began to realize my love for triathlons was fading. I didn't know how to handle these feelings. How do I go about telling people I no longer have a desire to train for or do triathlons, when it's what I had identified myself with nearly my entire life? For a little while, I continued training and acting as if nothing was wrong, but deep down I knew that triathlons weren't the same for me as they used to be. The hardest person for me to face during this time was Steve. I loved Steve so much that I didn't have the heart or the courage at the time to tell him how I was truly feeling about triathlons. I was embarrassed by the fact that what I had aspired to do my entire life was now nothing more than a hassle, with me dreading every training session I had to go to.

This all came to a climax the summer before senior year, when I informed my parents and Steve that I no longer intended on swimming in college, as I had originally planned. With this decision, my attending Team Total Training practices came to an abrupt halt. Ever since then, Steve and I have had little to no communication, and this is nobody's fault but my own. I want to take this time out to apologize to Steve, and to let him know how sorry I am for acting the way I did. The last thing I wanted was for things to work out the way they did between us, I just didn't want to disappoint him. I got tired of all the training and traveling that went into triathlons, and after so many years of it, I felt like I just wasn't having fun anymore. I wanted to spend more time being around my school friends, and eventually I realized that triathlons were no longer one of my top priorities. Also, the added pressure I felt from my dad left me questioning whose dream it was I was living out. Looking back, I know there were thousands of ways I probably could have handled the situation better.

Unfortunately, I can't change what already happened, but this is my first step in attempting to make it better. Thank you for everything you've ever done for me Steve. Words can't describe how thankful I am to have met someone like you. Your guidance and support throughout my entire life have helped get me to where I am now. I can't imagine how drastically different my life would be had I not met you. Nothing can take away from all the amazing time we've spent together and, hopefully, there are many more good times to come. You will always be a second father to me Steve, and hopefully we can see each other soon to catch up. Again, thank you for everything. I hope all is well with Jean and the bunnies. See you soon!

Michael Stewart's Thank You Letter to Steve

Dear Steve,

Where do I even start? The amount of things I have to thank you for cannot be summarized in a simple letter, but I'll give it my best shot.

Thank you for giving me the chance to swim with all the adults at your Team Total Training practices before there was a real place for kids to train. Without these practices, it is questionable that I ever would have fallen in love with triathlons the way that I did.

Next, I would like to thank you for creating the Team Total Training junior division. The junior team gave me a time and place to share my love for the sport of triathlon with other girls and boys my age. I am still friends with many of my fellow junior triathletes to this very day. Without you, I never would have been given the opportunity to meet these people.

Finally, and most importantly, I would like to thank you for being the role model you were to me. I've looked up to you since the first day I ever met you, Steve. What you did, taking me under your wing, driving me all over Long Island, mentoring me and giving me advice along the way, is something I'll never be able to thank you enough for. Your kindness, generosity, and wisdom instilled in me lifelong values I intend to pass onto my own kids one day.

You will always be a second father to me, Steve, nothing in the world will ever change that. Without your guidance, I really don't think I'd be where I am today.

Thanks again for everything that you've done for me. I hope you and Jean have a happy, healthy Thanksgiving. See you soon!

Love Always,

Michael Stewart

Chapter Four

Through the
Eyes
of the
Community

CHAPTER FOUR

"He was a teacher, a leader, an innovator; a
friend all from the kindness of his heart.
Steve was the endless cup of giving."
—Wendy Ingraham

It is important that Steve's story is told from the eyes of those closest to him. But it's equally as important to know how colleagues and fellow athletes felt about him. I have collected quotes from those who were touched by Steve's life in some positive way.

Steve was involved in the sport of triathlon from its beginnings in the early 1980s. He was first an athlete, then later a coach and event director. In every stage of his involvement, Steve developed a great reputation and was well respected by numerous legends of the sport. When I requested a quote from these accomplished people (some of whom I have not met, or met only a few times) for this memoir, I thought for sure their response would be, "Jean who?" Instead, not only was I given a quote, but many of them said they would be honored to be a part of the book. Even though I knew Steve was so loved and respected by many, I was still blown away.

The second part of this chapter has a representation of several quotes from over a hundred that were left on a tribute page to Steve in the Slowtwitch community (www.slowtwitch.com). Slowtwitch is the who's who of triathlon websites for triathletes from around the world, including beginners, age groupers, and professionals. Some of the tributes to Steve are from people I know, while more than half are from people I have never met.

It is human nature to always say good things about the deceased. However, in Steve's case, I believe the detailed and specific sentiments expressed by so many that are in this chapter speak volumes about the remarkable impact Steve had on so many lives.

From Legends of the Sport

Steve Tarpinian was one of the few men I know who was so comfortable in his own skin he could get away with wearing a sarong. And damn did he look good in one! —Rip Esselstyn

Steve was one of the most inspiring people I have ever known. His low key nature and strong work ethic set the tone for my own coaching business for the entire time I knew him. It was always fun racing with him, doing his races, but what I mostly remember was the great times we had after the races! His indomitable will and level headed consistency guide my life, even though he has left us, I feel his spirit still! —John Howard

My fondest memory of Steve was the pure joy he seemed to experience with such a seemingly simple act as, for example, swimming to the coast guard buoy in Kona. He took none of that for granted. And he shared that joy with me many times. —Michael Lovato

Met him many times. He was our race director in New York when Jim Curl and I brought back the USTS in the late 1990s. I never saw the demons, just a handsome, vigorous, hard-working guy, dedicated to the sport and to his job as race director, with an incredibly loyal following in the New York Metro area. I remember him smiling a lot – a big genuine grin that came from deep inside. He was an all-in kind of guy, although in retrospect, perhaps he was all in it for other folks and not enough for himself. It's hard to figure. I guess confidence is something we take for granted in triathlon. You see it, accept it, move on. Who in this business dares to wear their vulnerabilities on their sleeves? Who takes time to really listen? I'm an old guy now, so it's easy for me to say, but perhaps we should all slow down a bit and do just that: listen. Maybe that would have helped. Maybe not. Steve was a good guy. He should still be with us. —Mike Plant

When Steve Tarpinian passed away the Triathlon world truly lost an incredible, wonderful, passionate man. He gave so much to so many for so many years. He was the "Quiet Man" who had incredible energy and love for sport; as a coach, an event director, athlete, accomplished writer, family man, and as a fellow human being on this planet. Steve, you touched thousands and you will forever live in our hearts! Thank you for all that you gave in your ever so brief time with us. You will never ever be forgotten my friend! Thank you for YOU man! —Whit Raymond

My greatest and most consistent memory of Steve is that he always had a singular focus on whomever he was speaking to. When we collided, it was never about him. He had a genuine humanistic and compassionate interest in what I was doing. Never a notion of any ego, just a very humble and sincere gentlemen. In watching Steve with his athletes, everyone was treated equally and with an uncanny respect and warmth. This was the Steve that I remember. I was deeply saddened as I was with Robin Williams, whom I knew; that Steve did not have the outlet to share his inner pain. —Dave Scott

I didn't really know Steve well and would never claim to; the pieces of others engaged in competitive grieving serving as a reminder of just how f****** shallow and self-serving we can be even within other's turmoil. But dammit if he ain't gone too young and for the wrong reasons so why not pretend. Or at least come to grips with what he tried to be. Which was a simple guy who wanted to help and wanted to be loved if not admired for wanting to help. Steve taught people how to swim. Now, correct me if I'm wrong but if you don't drown and you go on to inspire others or bank a fortune or foster a family or clean your gutters or find the cure for cancer or pick up a piece of trash or teach others to swim because one guy with a long tall pony ticking away on the pool deck as if some perfect metronome enabled you...then what is so wrong with that life? There was nothing wrong with Steve's life. It was a beautiful thing. Only problem was...he didn't know it soon enough. —Scott Tinley

I don't quite remember when I first met Steve, but I am pretty sure it was in the early 90's in Kona. Always with a wry smile on his face and a head full of hair, tucked back in a ponytail, much to my envy! We always enjoyed a quiet chat whether talking about swim coaching on the big island or how many races he had done that year! Depression is a very common disease, one that I know very well having suffered myself after a series of debilitating heart surgeries, (12) and having to recover from each one of them differently. Problem for me was that they were saving my life but I didn't know how to move forward in life after being a pro triathlete for 12 years. I too have suffered enormous loss through suicide. My uncle lost his life over 15 years ago and it was only two years ago that I lost my dear nephew. Then the unbelievable happened, my good friend Robin Williams had suffered as well. The news of Steve's passing in March rocked the Triathlon and swimming world of Kona, Maui, Long Island and the global sporting communities. I paused for a moment in reflection of all the great things he did in his life, and the long lasting legacy that has been left behind with the knowledge that he shared amongst our vast friendships. Steve may you rest in peace and I will see you again. —Greg Welch

From The Slowtwitch Community

Steve was the best friend I had in the sport of triathlon and one of the best in my life. We both had a passion for the sport but he made it fun. We were buddies that cracked each other up, fans that argued about who were the best athletes, what were the best races, what was the best way to train, but most of all Steve was to me and countless others, an inspiration. I remember telling him how proud and amazed I was of him because he could turn his passion, talent and understanding of his sport into a successful living and life style. While the rest of us had to put on a suit and tie and take the train into the office, Steve traveled the world doing what he loved and helping so many people along the way. Swim fast up there Tarp. As usual, I'm way behind you — in a wetsuit. —Chuck Sperazza

Steve was my beloved coach, mentor and hero. Although I only got to work with him and race with Team Total Training for a brief year, he left a profound impact on my life. His grace and guidance helped to lift me out of a postpartum depression, gave me the courage and skills to race triathlons, and encouraged me to begin teaching cycling here in Maine. I am deeply saddened by his passing, but hopeful that he has finally found the peace he was looking for. I am forever grateful for the wonderful coaching I received, the fantastic people he introduced me to, and mostly for the beautiful memories he passed on to those of us who had the privilege of knowing him. Steve was larger than life, an icon in the sport of triathlon. Rest in peace, dear coach. —Amy Herschl Pillitteri

As a young triathlete, I had the privilege of life guarding with Steve at the beach. We immediately bonded over the sport we loved, and he inspired me to push myself and be the best I could be. I later became a coach, following Steve's example of giving back to the sport he loved in any way he could. Steve will live on in all of us as Legend, as an athlete, as a coach, and as a friend. —Matt Winkler

A few years back, he and I were both at Ironman Lake Placid. Steve had raced, and I was just there to work and do some training. The day after the race I was out riding my bike, and I accidentally found myself mixed in with the weekly Monday Night Mini Tri that takes place all summer long. As I was pedaling along, Steve came flying by me in the race. The day before he had completed his tenth Ironman Lake Placid in a row, yet there he was doing a super sprint triathlon - and having a blast! I sprinted up to him, rode alongside him, and said "Hi." Then I asked why he was doing the race. Most people sit on their butts the day after an Ironman. Steve just looked at me and beamed that power smile and said "There was a perfectly good triathlon taking place, and I needed a cool down." Simple as that. I rode next to him for a few more minutes, just enough time for him to admit it probably wasn't going to feel very good during the run, and then he sped off, happy as can be. That's how I remember Steve: smiling all the time, doing the sport of triathlon because it was fun, and because there was no better reason than that. —Michael Lovato

His smile danced with excitement, his eyes light up like the stars in the night when he was making someone shine. He was a teacher, a leader, an innovator, a friend all from the kindness of his heart, Steve was the endless cup of giving. He left behind a space we must fix, he taught us how to make it better and brighter. Now is the time to not be sad but to show Steve we can shine together. There will be no more loneliness, we are a triathlon community, we are strong, and we must help one another. The time has come, the time is now to fight the demon of depression. This will keep Steve shining bright above us. —Wendy Ingraham

I will never forget you Steve. Mighty North Fork 2002 was my first triathlon. I was ecstatic to be a part of an event that epitomized a complete life change for me. Thanks to your love and support you made me feel a part of the team. You and Team Total Training accepted me with open arms and saw an athlete in me that I had never imagined could exist. You looked beyond my limitations and saw only possibilities and the strength I had to accomplish them. I regret that I never got the chance to tell you this — I pray that you feel the love and that you rest in eternal peace. —Spiro Hamilothoris

Mighty Hamptons Olympic Triathlon in 1995 was my first triathlon ever. Steve was an instrumental support in mine and my husband's first Ironman in Florida in 2000, and was there at the finish line in Kona for David when he won his age group in 2001, we had no clue, Steve was in the media tent and came running out waving the print outs of the results to tell Dave that he won. With David's success through my plan, Steve took me under his wing. Back then, online coaching was non-existent. I had faxed, or mailed hand written plans to triathletes I coached. I was there at the start of Steve's Total Training University (TTU), and Steve introduced me to online coaching while allowing me to have free rein and control, with his full trust and confidence in me, of the online athletes that came through TTU. I had the pleasure of collaborating with him on early sprint through half iron programs that we spiral bound and mailed to athletes that purchased them from TTU. I still have the first prototype in my desk. Steve encouraged, motivated and helped people to realize their own dreams. He was a mentor to me, he built a great culture of triathlon racing on Long Island. I don't think of him as a swim coach or a triathlon coach or a race director. He was a life coach without knowing it. Thank you Steve for passing on your enthusiasm and posi-

tivity and I can't help but notice that for those who have been touched by you, all continue to spread that message. —Jenny Gatz

The year was 1996. I was 36 yrs old. I had just boldly decided to "do the Ironman," while watching the epic Thomas Hellriegel-Mark Allen battle from 1995 Kona Ironman. All great, right? Well, except for one small problem. I had had a near drowning as a child, hadn't been in water any deeper than waist deep, was scared to death of it, and knew absolutely zero about how to become a swimmer. Enter "Swim Power" on VHS and my decision to attend Steve's workshop out in Long Island. I was in awe of him that day, in part because of his charisma and of course his awesome swimming ability (evident in that opening footage from Swim Power!). From the moment I met him and he welcomed me like an old friend, he was patient, encouraging, positive and smiling, and helped me, along with many others, learn some of the basic swim skills that would become the cornerstone for continued learning to this day. It was that day that I first learned of the importance of flexibility for swimming (something I lacked) - he exposed us all to the "Fraid Not" ropes to enhance that upper body flexibility - a tool I continue to use and recommend to others to this day. I consider Steve to be among my MOST important mentors and influencers in my triathlon journey. Of course, while we all know Steve was a GREAT teacher, what I most remember and cherish about having had the honor to learn from him, was the smile he shared with me whenever we would run into each other, at races or later on at coaching conferences. He always treated me as an equal and always had a positive word of encouragement. He was humble, wicked smart and way ahead of his time as a coach, and as so many have said, one of those people who just made you feel good and welcomed, whenever you saw him. I think, like so many others who learned from him and saw him every so often....I did not know of his struggle with depression. I think I'm most disappointed now, that I didn't say "thank you" enough times, to him. I really believe in my heart that the world is not quite the same without him, as it was with him. And that saddens me. But he left a legacy and set a standard for us all to live up to, of giving, sharing, smiling, hoping, believing, and then giving, again. Thank you, Steve. Thank you. May you rest in peace my friend. —Al Lyman

Carolyn and I did MightyMan Triathlon a few years back and Steve's enthusiasm made a small, low key race feel like the biggest of events. It was the first race that we won together, and Steve made it feel like it was truly a big deal. I've never been to a race where my presence felt so truly appreciated, and I know it wasn't just because I did well - he made everyone there that day feel like a winner. The sport will definitely miss him. —Brian MacIlvain

I did not compete in any triathlons with Steve, he never trained me and I was not in that world, however, I must say beyond that arena he was a true gentleman as well. I recall working with him when I was at the beach in my college years (he was a bit older). He treated his younger co-workers with respect and kindness. I distinctly remember complaining to him before my senior year that I was sick of swimming and he said, "It is all over before you know it and you will never get that chance again, don't waste it." I remember that conversation clearly, he was right and every time I have the same conversation with another young athlete I think of him. I am sorry for the family's loss. He will be remembered by me fondly. —Casey Murphy

Steve and I met swimming for the Mid-Nassau YMCA Stingrays in the mid 70's. We also swam together at Chaminade high school. He was the senior co-captain and I was a freshman who was moved up to varsity after the freshman season ended. I remember some of the older guys resenting me on varsity but not Steve. He made us feel welcome and invited me to my first swim team keg party. I guess my parents were okay with underage drinking as long as they knew Steve was there. He encouraged me and many others to take the Jones Beach lifeguard test which was one of the best decisions of my life. He was one of the best guards on the beach and often won the pool swim event at the annual Jones Beach races. When we were scheduled to sit together on main stands or wing stands, I looked forward to it. My condolences to Steve's many friends and family. They say you can judge a man's life by the number and quality of the friends he had. Steve was a very wealthy guy in that regard. —Jim O'Connnor

Steve is the reason why I do what I do today in endurance sports. He got me into triathlons and never once allowed me or others to not put in our best effort. He was always smiling and was the first to give a handshake and a warm hello. My family and I will sorely miss him, he was like a father figure and someone I looked up to for being an all around great person. He is obviously a legend in the triathlon community, especially on Long Island. Without him triathlon would certainly not be what it is today. Thank you for all that you did for me and everyone. We love and miss you dearly. —Matthew Korsky

This man ate, slept and breathed training knowledge and coaching...a fine athlete himself, he took to coaching like most people take to breathing. While I never worked with him, a former running club mate of mine was one of Steve's many protégés and Steve brought out the very best in him, coaching him in every aspect of the triathlon game. He truly bonded with his athletes, respected them, cared about them and nurtured them. The joy he got out of my friend's successes was palpable. And he was generous, rewarding my friend with a spa session at a high end local inn after his race in Lake Placid. I will always remember how he picked us up on a bike ride back from Montauk. His knowledge of the back roads of the East End was unsurpassed and he wove us through some beautiful spots before getting us back on the main road. If you train for anything and you knew Steve, train hard and finish your race with a smile on your face to honor what he was all about. A terrible tragedy that he is gone. —Alan Gardner

I did not know Steve on a personal basis but have done my share of triathlons on Long Island. I always admired the positive vibe and aura he emitted. He was constantly encouraging everyone that he came in contact with. He will be truly missed. My thoughts and prayers go out to his family, friends and loved ones. —Joseph Marino

As one of the only US Paralympics Pool racers, Steve took on the difficult task of specialized workouts for me. We became fast friends and he knew exactly how hard and far to push me. At the end of the workouts, he would help to gently lift me onto the pool deck. He was by my side for my comeback race last November where we laughed, and yet he got me in the zone and steadied me on the blocks. I always wanted to do my best for him. Everyone did. He brought that out of you. Only Steve could get a physically messed up sprinter, like me to enter Tri-Relays! I will continue to compete in them, in his honor. I know I will see him again. God will see to it. Thank you and I love you Steve. —Nancy Burpee

Saying a prayer for Steve and condolences to his family. One of those rare individuals that could make you feel special with a only brief connection. Because of that, I always thought of him as a mentor when I began triathlon racing on Long Island in 1999 eventually attending his swim coaching at SUNY Westbury and racing in several of his race-directed events. At 56, I finished my first Ironman triathlon last year and was hoping to reconnect with him and thank him for infusing me with his passion for the sport - I hoped to return to do a Long Island race this summer after leaving 14 years ago. Very sad. —David Krysh

Didn't know Steve well but knew him for a long time and long enough to know that he was one of the good guys. He always respected his fellow humans and in turn they appreciated this and respected him. He worked hard with a smile. It's a shame to learn of his depression because there is no one here who would not have helped this guy to overcome what ailed him and unfortunately ails many in this day and age. He loved and learned and not for naught. —Bruce Lulla

Steve gave me an instant community when I arrived on Long Island. Fun, supportive, and encouraging, he helped me to be a part of something I had never been exposed to - adults having fun, working out and working together. He helped me to realize that I could do so much more if I believed in myself. My heart breaks for his pain and for the loss for his family and this incredible community that he created. We will miss you, Beefy T. —Petra Trunkes

Rest in peace, Steve. I took my first triathlon swim lesson with him 7 years ago. I still remember it like it was yesterday. Newcomers will never get a chance to experience his enthusiasm, passion, and support... sadness all over :-(God bless :-(—Anita Caruso

Chapter Five

Through
His
Eyes

CHAPTER FIVE

"Many times as we look back on the absurdity
of our existence, it helps us appreciate the here
and now and many wonders of life."
—Steve Tarpinian

Steve was a prolific writer throughout his life, whether it be his published works on swimming and/or training, or his musings and observations about life in general. There is no better way to see Steve than through his very own words. In this chapter, I have included some of his published and unpublished writings.

Poetry

Steve's poem, "The Spiritual Athlete," was composed in 1986 and he described it as his definition of a real man.

"The Spiritual Athlete"

He is strong,
He fights long,
When life is tough;
He accepts it and brushes it off his cuff.

The real man knows the power of the mind,
And that being macho is being kind.
Anyone can work their body and perform phenomenal athletic feats.
But in reality, the real man is the spiritual athlete,
And in the end when we are all reduced to dust,
The spiritual athlete is the only one who prevails,
And lasts forever.

The next two handwritten poems, "Soul Mates" (1988) and "Ode to the Princess" (1991), I found in birthday cards he had given me.

Ode to the Princess

How does one explain;
a princess who calms pain;
not from an incident of frivolity;
but that pain of anonimity;
There are doctors + drugs
to alleviate pain from the flesh;
but I am talking about the inner soul
and the difficulty of making it feel fresh;
fresh as in a morning when day is whole;

Often times I am so very scared;
I feel as though I am being dared;
to step outside myself and be a man,
The princess makes me believe I can;

As if this is not enough;
the princess's name is more beautiful than
one of montauks bluffs;

Manella How can a man such as I, not love

Soul mates   San Diego Area,

As they peered out over the Southern California
He pulled her close,
His intent was an over dose,
This hug was very symbolic;
Love untested by time is lust,
It takes time to earn and receive trust.

They embraced for a long moment
and felt their hearts in sync; could be no limit.
For this moment in time the ~~some limit~~.

When hearts beat as one
they beat stronger apart.

The Writings of a Coach

Below is a 2010 "race report" where Steve reflects his thoughts on a local triathlon in which he participated; his reflections were sent to all the members of his triathlon team.

I would love to report that I had an awesome race this weekend. I felt good the week leading in. I had some good prep sessions and felt rested; in short, all systems were go! I always really enjoy this race but not because of the race itself; the water is not the cleanest, there is a crazy, rough swim start, and a there is a dangerous bike course with cars. However, I do love the run which is nice and hilly. I also like this race because we have so many teammates that the camaraderie is off the hook! I especially love the swim start when I get a chance to hug and wish all my buddies good luck before the race starts and we proceed to froth up the water. Well, just before the race start I was thinking this is going to be a great race for me, I was feeling good. To summarize, I had a mediocre race, not terrible, but definitely not great. I realized it right from the start; when I was getting beat up in the first 100 yards and could not seem to jump out in front with the leaders like I usually can do. BTW, if you did not know it, the front of the swim is many times as bad and rough as mid or back of the pack. There are too many swimmers all trying to lead the race, most cannot but for 100 - 200 yards, the ones that cannot make it grueling for the ones that can before they start to fall behind. Anyway, I realized at that moment, for whatever reason, my body was not as ready to perform as well as my mind was thinking it would be. The rest of the race went similar, I kept thinking; okay, stay positive, you have been here before and sometimes it takes time to get in the groove and even if the groove never comes, enjoy the day, the people, the teammates and simply the fact we can do what we do. Well, the groove never came so I plodded along doing the best I could and was happy to be able to cross the finish line and get hugs and high fives from teammates. I was really excited to see how well our top athletes did. Damn, it seemed everyone had a solid race. Probably the most exciting finish for me was when one teammate came in after having to fix her own flat tire on the bike!

Why, may you ask, am I writing a race report for a so-so race? Jean encouraged me to, after I shared with her my surprise I did not perform as fast as I thought I would and yet still felt I performed well for how my body was responding on the day. She said, "Write a report, your teammates will be inspired that even an experienced athlete like you sometimes has days that they just are not on... and that it is okay." I said, "You're right."

So my friends, as always, the beauty is in the balance. There are going to be more races and more opportunities to perform better (whatever that really means anyway). Being able to stay present and enjoy whatever is dealt you on race day... a good lesson for us all and a lesson I have re-learned a few times. Of course, going to the Team Party after the race was certainly a blast and quickly reminded me why I do this sport in the first place, no one parties like a triathlete! Only at a triathlon party will you find a drinking game going on and half the players are drinking water! Of course the ones drinking beer did better!

Books

In 2005, Steve published *The Triathlete's Guide to Swim Training.* I have included some excerpts here.

When I left my job as an electrical engineer 20 years ago to become a swim and triathlon coach, I (and others) thought I was crazy. Not only did I leave a lucrative career, but I also dove into a field that did not yet exist. The main reason why I made the change was that I realized my desire to be around athletes and help them reach their goals. I did not know that these same athletes would help me reach mine. This book and any of my other creations in the field of coaching would not be possible without all the athletes whom I have had the good fortune to coach. I wish I could have another volume to list all your names, but you know who you are. Thanks!

When I was 12 years old, I started swimming year-round. I was below average for my swim club, but I was an above average baseball player. At 14, I felt I needed to choose between being a competitive swimmer and a baseball player. It was a hard decision, made worse by the fact that my swim coach suggested I stay with baseball! When I finally made up my mind, I realized I was choosing swimming for the challenge of it and my love for the sport. I was out to be the best I could be.

Most recently, Steve wrote a book, *Resurrection*, about his grandmother—a survivor of the 1915 Armenian Massacre. Below is the preface of that book. He finished the manuscript for this book the week before he passed away.

How many times have we all said, "Was I lucky! If that accident had happened any other way, I wouldn't be here!" This "what if" line of thinking can be taken to any extreme. It can certainly be carried back to our ancestors, our very existence. Many times as we look back on the absurdity of our existence, it helps us appreciate the here and now and many wonders of life.

My Grandmother, Hripsime (Armenian for Helen) survived the Armenian Massacre of 1915. Her stories have often inspired me to reach for the seemingly unattainable. The combination of her unwavering will to survive and sheer luck gives me the feeling that her survival is a gift from God. I feel grateful to be her grandson, and I feel her story of survival is an inspiration to everyone.

What follows is a chronological story of her trek from Sivas (Turkey) to Aleppo (Syria) and eventually, her escape to America. There is some history of the Turkish-Armenian conflict for those unfamiliar with the genesis of the Armenian genocide. The description of her journey is from her memory of over 60 years before I interviewed her, and my attempt to tie together all of her stories. I hope that all who read this feel her strength. One of the things my grandmother prayed for (and it's a lengthy list) is peace on earth. It is sad that as I put the finishing touches on this story, bloodshed of many forms is still very much a part of life throughout the world. Sometimes it is difficult to be optimistic. Hopefully this story inspires more peace and compassion to those who read it and share it. One of Hitler's most powerful and telling quotes regarding the atrocities he planned and committed during World War II was when, on August 22, 1939, he said, "Who, after all, speaks today of the annihilation of the Armenians?"

My reason for starting this project was merely to learn about my grandmother's life. For as long as I can remember I was told these incredible stories of the Armenian massacre, and how a few people, including my grandmother, had survived against tremendous odds. I was dissatisfied with small sections of the story--I wanted to know more. After I started the project, I realized other people would be moved to read about the survival of the human body and spirit. What you are about to read is based on a true story. The events take place between 1903 and 1940.

Steve was a true Renaissance man. Before his career as a coach, athlete, and race director, he was an electrical engineer designing Automatic Test Equipment for the Grumman F14 fighter jets. Throughout all of this time, Steve thought of himself primarily as a writer. Many times, when Steve had to enter his occupation on a race registration form, he would say writer. Perhaps after you finish this chapter, you can see why Steve identified himself as such. What follows is my favorite of all of Steve's writings: *A Mouse In the House.*

This short story personifies the kindness and gentleness of Steve Tarpinian.

a Mouse
in the
House

A short story by Steve Tarpinian

Illustrations
by
Steve
Dansereau

FOREWORD

In 2012, Hurricane Sandy devastated countless human lives, many of whom are still recovering in 2015. Steve and I considered ourselves very lucky; the only damage we sustained was a tree falling and destroying our back-yard shed.

There are also many untold stories of how non-human species were adversely impacted by Hurricane Sandy. One such story is of mice that sought refuge in our home. Steve and I believed that the mice were also casualties of Hurricane Sandy, as we thought they must have fled from our shed in terror to the closest safe place—our house. These mice inspired Steve to write the true story *A Mouse in the House.*

The lesson in this story is to show compassion. Some of us are more fragile than others and need to be handled with care. Depression has many faces and you would never think some people have this illness. Showing compassion is not a sign of weakness. It is a sign of great strength of character and a powerful human spirit. Steve showed great compassion for the little critters in this story. He had a great capacity for love and compassion for all living beings in his life. That is what made him a giant among men.

"You can easily judge the character of a man by how he treats those who can do nothing for him." —Author Unknown.

a Mouse

in the

House

A short story by Steve Tarpinian

Illustrations
by
Steve
Dansereau

I had seen mice in the pet store.

These little creatures were adorable and on sale for only ninety ninety-cents each. They were small,and seemed to be sleeping all over themselves. They were extremely cute.

"What a good pet they could make," I thought to myself. "They're small, quiet, vegetarians and smart!"

Then I realized I had no extra time
to devote to any pets in addition to the
two rescued rabbits Jean and I owned.

What was I going to do with a mouse anyway? Take him for a run? Teach him how to swim or ride a bike? Oh well, I said good-bye to the little fellas and hoped they did not end up being fed to someone's snake. I didn't think about mice again until Hurricane Sandy.

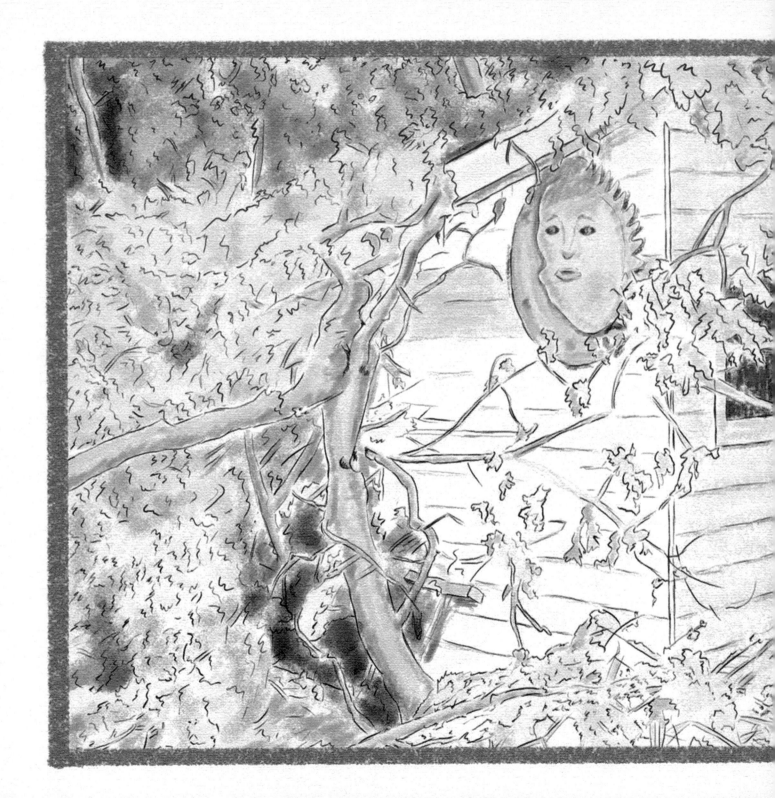

There were many devastating stories two days after the hurricane when I returned home from a trip. Luckily there were not a lot of fatalities, but thousands of people were left without a home they could live in and hundreds with literally no home at all. One sad story I heard was of a woman who, as she was closing her door to the rising water saw several small mice swimming towards the door trying to get in. I never asked if the women let the little guys in, frankly I didn't want to know. That made me realize how many little animals were also displaced. Sad story, but with so much to do helping friends clean up after the storm and stay warm with no heat and electricity at our home, I did not dwell much on the story of the swimming mice.

We were very lucky. The only damage at our house was from a big tree that fell from a neighbor's yard and took down one of our trees on its way to crushing our cute little shed. Our neighbor Danny was so worried about it that he would fix it for us and get the tree removed. We assured him we were not worried one bit and he need not worry. He was relieved and we were happy to see him smile. He has always been a terrific neighbor and friend to us for over ten years.

As the days passed, things started to get a little crazy with gas lines forming at the gas stations, an unexpected snow storm and delays on getting power and cable service back to hundreds of thousands of homes like ours. These natural disasters tend to bring out the best and worst in people. Some people had fights on gas lines while others opened their homes to neighbors and friends. A friend of ours named Josie was staying with us since her condominium was flooded. Ironically, it was Josie's neighbor who told her the story of the mice trying to swim to her door.

As the weeks passed by, life slowly started to get back to normal. The gas lines receded, people were starting to return to their homes, but it seemed to go very slowly. One day, I went into the kitchen in the morning and saw a small black "thing" scurry into the bottom of the kitchen cabinet. I say black "thing" since I really feel like all I saw was a tail wiggle around and then disappear.

I froze in place wondering if I really saw this or if I was still asleep and imagining it? I knelt down to see where it went and sure enough, in one corner of the cabinet there was an open space where there was no wood about three inches wide. I was now convinced that I saw a mouse as he ran back into his hiding place. Was there a mouse in the house? Should I tell Jean and our houseguest Josie? I let them know what I saw and the mystery mouse became a daily topic of conversation.

A few days later Josie left us a note that said, "I think the mouse ate some of this bread". Jean and I looked and saw a small tear into a paper bag that had some bread in it and a small bite was missing. In addition we saw a few small droppings on the counter. Jean was angry and said now they are invading our space and eating our food. We have to do something. I said, "Oh what's the harm?" She explained to me that they can carry all sorts of disease and multiply and so on.

The next day, as Jean and I were discussing how we would handle this problem, Josie told us that she saw the mouse as well. That day we also found more evidence of the rummaging they were up to when we found a wrapper from a chocolate bar all torn up and wedged in one of our stove burners. And there was another problem - Josie described a white and brown mouse, and I saw a black one. We no longer had a mouse problem we had a mice problem!

That was the last straw. Jean said they have to go.

We decided we would get mousetraps and I said I would take care of the task the next day.   It was a very busy day of work with meetings and driving around, phone calls, etc. I told a neighbor, Bob, that we had a mice problem and his response was go to Home Depot to get some mouse traps. Although I felt reassured I could get the right things to take care of the problem, I knew he was not talking about anything close to humane. I was off to buy traps to rid us of the mice. My phone rang as I was entering Home Depot and it was Jean asking if I got the traps yet and to get humane ones. I assured her I would do my best to get humane traps and that I was walking in to get them at that very moment. After getting the other supplies I was there for, I asked a Home Depot employee where I could get mousetraps. He said row nine and as I started to walk in that direction he said "make sure you get the old fashioned ones, the humane ones don't work". I looked over the shelves trying to see if there were any humane options. They all looked and sounded lethal. I was running out of time and settled myself to the fact I was getting the ones that will solve the problem. Off I went, made my purchases and headed home.

As soon as I got home, Bob and I went to work putting peanut butter on the traps and setting them in the cabinets and on the floor where we had seen the mice. Jean asked if the mouse would suffer and Bob said no, not at all. Then when she left the room, he leaned toward me and in a soft voice said, "they usually do not die right away and the box will flip around, so you just take them out and "finish them off". Great, I get to be the one to grab the mouse twisting in pain and take him out to "finish him off".

That evening, while having dinner, the subject of these traps came up. Jean wanted to be sure that if we hear one in the night that I would get up and take care of it. The reality that the traps would kill the mice had settled in, and I realized that I am not okay with that.

I started to do a search on the computer for humane traps. As with anything else, there is a wealth of information on the Internet for trapping mice. I found all types of traps and their reviews. It appeared as though some of them do work.

A few sounded like they were not much better than the killer ones but I did find one that is a large metal box and has two openings that the mouse can go in, but once in, they can't get out. The description says it can trap up to thirty mice! I called the local Ace and Home Depot stores. It was now 8:30 PM. I was running out of time and at any moment I might hear the a snap of the trap just a few feet away from me. A store nearby that closes at 9:00 PM said they have the trap I want in stock. I asked Josie and Jean, who had just finished eating dinner and were looking over my shoulder while I was researching, if we should run out and get this trap.

It was unanimous. I got ready to go, Jean took the inhumane traps away and washed off the peanut butter, and Josie said she would take a ride with me. Thirty dollars later, we were checking out of the hardware store and on the way home.

We loaded the trap with three whole wheat crackers, some gourmet peanut butter, and cheese. There were holes in the side of the trap so the aroma of these delicacies could waft out and attract the mice. Ah, relief, we could all sleep knowing we were not going to hear a "snap" and come in to see a dead little animal in the kitchen.

The next day we decided to call an exterminator to get a professional opinion of how to handle mouse infestation. That afternoon, a very knowledgeable and nice guy from a large company that handles all sorts of critter infestations (mice, rats, squirrels, raccoons etc.) took a flashlight and searched around the area where we saw the mice. The exterminator found another area with some evidence of mice activity (in other words, droppings) under the stove. He then took a walk around the house to see if there were any areas that mice could come in from the outside. When he returned, he sat down to give us his results and suggestions for handling the situation. The exterminator advised us to seal off some small exterior openings where a mouse could gain access to the house.

After a few days with no takers in the trap and no sign of mice we started to wonder if they had left on their own. We had, however, spoken with many friends and acquaintances that had dealt with mice in the past and not one of them told us that the problem was solved without having to trap them, or worse, "finish them off".

A few days later, I had some trouble sleeping and sat up in the living room watching TV. I thought I heard a rattling in the kitchen. I muted the TV and there was silence. I started to fall asleep so I went back into the bedroom. A few hours later one of our rabbits started thumping. We also heard some more rattling in the kitchen. Jean and I headed to the kitchen and there was no noise.

I decided to take a look inside the trap with a flashlight just in case there was a mouse and every time he thought we were around, he stopped stirring. Sure enough, I saw two little eyes staring back at me!

"We caught one!" I shouted, "and it's a baby!"

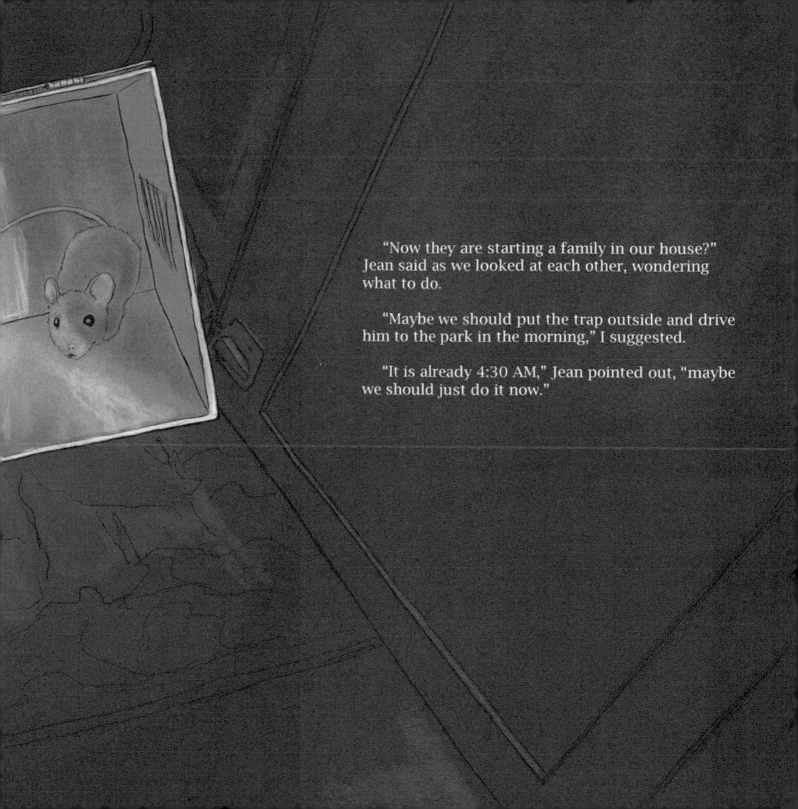

"Now they are starting a family in our house?"
Jean said as we looked at each other, wondering
what to do.

"Maybe we should put the trap outside and drive
him to the park in the morning," I suggested.

"It is already 4:30 AM," Jean pointed out, "maybe
we should just do it now."

The next thing I knew, we were in the car heading to a park that is exactly one and a half miles from our house. We needed to go more than a mile away, since the exterminator told us that if you take a mouse less than a mile away they would usually come back to the same house! We drove into the park, which was lit up from all the organizations doing recovery for Hurricane Sandy. It was surreal; lit like daytime and no one there.

We parked by the roadside near some bushes. I took the trap and set it down on the grass and as I slowly open the trap the cutest little mouse was staring back at us and looking very scared. He took a few steps toward us, stood up and seemed to be staring right at us. Jean said "Hi Peanut!" Then after a few more seconds he jumped out of the tin box and scurried into the hedges.

We got in the car and I said to Jean that he was too small and probably will not survive. She said, "Sure he will, he is a field mouse and belongs outside".

"I hope so," I told her, but inside, I felt he was just too frail. We both felt good he at least had a fighting chance, and headed home.

The next day we had a second exterminator come over. He smiled when we told him the story of Peanut. He said we did the right thing to have the entry points around the house closed. He also had some other types of humane traps and sold us three of them. Now we had not one but four humane traps set up and ready to catch more mice.

Days went by and nothing.

Maybe they were on to us?

Maybe they saw Peanut get caught and left town?

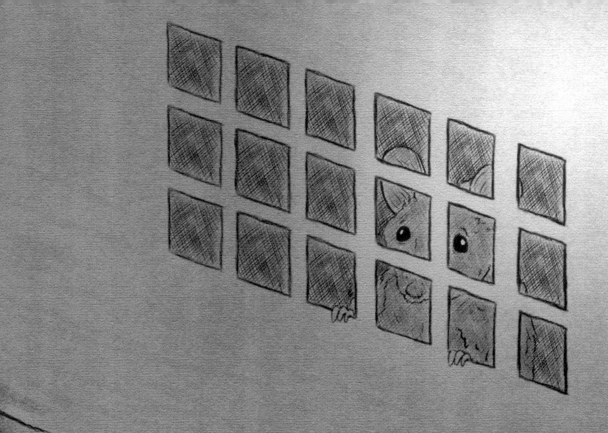

Not so fast.

A day or two later, I was out and received a message on my phone from Jean telling me that we caught another mouse in the new trap. Another baby!

On the message she asked me to come home and help her take care of it as soon as I could. I had a few meetings and the whole time I was thinking about how we could keep the mouse, maybe not as a pet, but at least for awhile, and at least until he can get bigger and stronger before we set him free to meet up with Peanut.

A few hours later, as I was finishing up my last meeting, Jean called and said, "Pipsqueak is really cute! How are we going to handle releasing him?"

Pipsqueak? I thought, this is not good, he now has a name and Jean is getting attached. "Maybe we should keep him," I suggested.

"No way!" she exclaimed - immediately followed by, "but if we do, make sure you get a wheel or something that he can exercise on."

Man, talk about mixed messages! She evidently looked up mice as pets online and they need things like that. "Don't worry," I told her, "I have a plan and will be home in an hour."

Plan? What plan? I have no plan. I simply know that I do not want to toss another little baby out in the now freezing weather to try and find his brother or sister and food and probably be chased and maybe caught by some wild cat or other predator. Mice are like rabbits in that they are prey animals. I stood in the parking lot getting ready to get in my car, and as I lifted my head I noticed a pet store.

That's the solution! I would go in and buy a small tank and we can keep the mouse for a few days, feed him and make him strong and then release him. I went in and spent forty dollars on a tank, screen top and an exercise wheel.

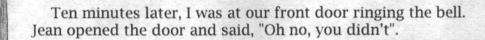

Ten minutes later, I was at our front door ringing the bell. Jean opened the door and said, "Oh no, you didn't".

"Oh yes I did."

We quickly went into the kitchen and transferred Pipsqueak to the new tank with some fresh hay, a toilet paper tube and the wheel. He ran right into the tube. We wondered if he was going to figure out how to use the wheel. We put a cracker with peanut butter and a bottle cap with water in the tank and went to bed.

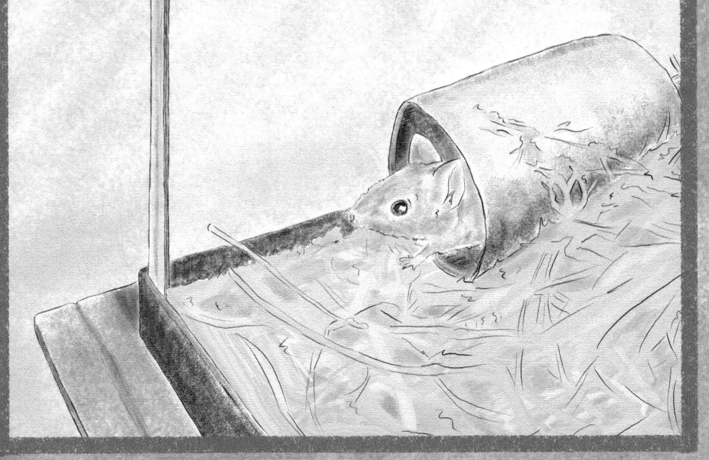

In the middle of the night I got up to get a drink and take a look in on Pipsqueak. As I approached the tank I could hear the wheel spinning!

Darn, in less than twelve hours, the food was gone and he was "in training". As I got close, he stopped and stared at me. This is what I saw - Pipsqueak after his first workout session!

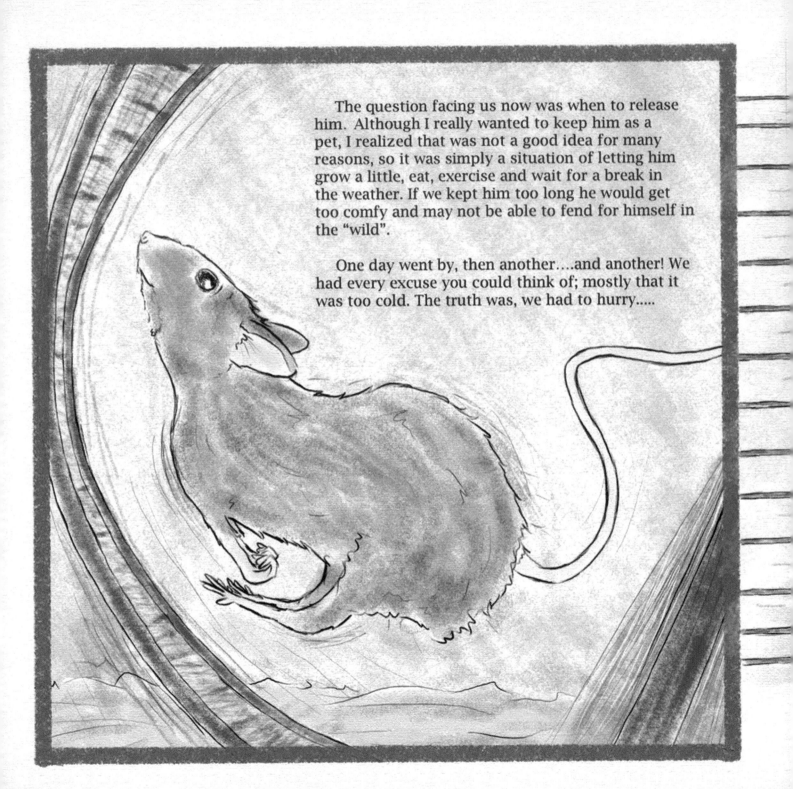

The question facing us now was when to release him. Although I really wanted to keep him as a pet, I realized that was not a good idea for many reasons, so it was simply a situation of letting him grow a little, eat, exercise and wait for a break in the weather. If we kept him too long he would get too comfy and may not be able to fend for himself in the "wild".

One day went by, then another....and another! We had every excuse you could think of; mostly that it was too cold. The truth was, we had to hurry.....

...because besides getting too comfy with the gourmet peanut butter and whole-wheat crackers, he was growing so fast that he was not fitting in his exercise wheel anymore!

When he did his exercise now, he would get tossed out after a few turns since his body was starting to span almost a quarter of the wheel.

Finally, after about four days, the sun came out and the weather warmed to about forty five degrees. It was time. We took the tank and drove over to Cedar Creek Park. We went to the same exact spot we released Peanut about two weeks earlier. Josie came with us and I slowly tilted the tank on its side. Pipsqueak hid in the hay for a little while, then he slowly started to walk out and once in the grass, darted into the hedges where we left Peanut.

Our fantasy is that he found his sibling and Peanut and Pipsqueak are frolicking around and enjoying the great outdoors.

And our mouse problem? It has been over two years and we have not seen another mouse in the house.

We keep the tank, just in case another one comes and we put him in the "catch and release" program that goes on at our little house in New York.

"Pipsqueak"

Chapter Six

Through
the
Lens

CHAPTER SIX

"The opposite of depression
is not happiness, but vitality."
—Andrew Solomon

A November/December 1999 article written for Bereavement (now Living With Loss) magazine ("Listen to our Stories") talked about "earthly angels." They were defined as friends, family members, and strangers who listen when we tell our stories about our loved ones. They support us in our efforts in learning how to live with, and manage, our grief.

This chapter is devoted to some of my fondest memories and the best times in my life with Steve. As painful as it was, putting this chapter together made me realize what a wonderful life I had with him.

Through the photos and anecdotes that follow, I hope you will see that a person suffering from depression can still have fulfilling and happy moments in his or her life, while creating many wonderful memories for others.

Meet the Parents, 1981

First Christmas together.

I was so afraid his parents would think I was a "cougar" (I don't remember what that was called over thirty years ago) as I was seven years older than Steve. My fears were unfounded. I was welcomed into their home and hearts with love. Steve loved to give me a hard time because I was eight years older than him for one month each year. My birthday is in November and his was in December. He made up for the ribbing, however, by celebrating my birthday with me for a full week and my wish was his command for that "birthday week."

Grandmother, 1987

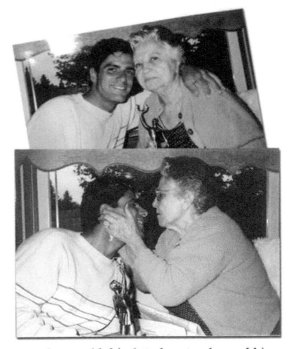

Every time Steve came home from a race, he would go to see his grandmother Marig. She would ask him, "Did you win Janus?" (Janus is an Armenian term of endearment). Steve would say, "No," and Marig would give a small harrumph. In 1987, Steve won the Town of Hempstead triathlon and was very excited to show Marig his trophy. As she always did, Marig asked, "Did you win Janus?" Steve finally could say, "Yes!" Marig promptly responded, "That's nice, Janus. Do you want some food?"

Steve with his 1st place trophy and his grandmother Marig (on his father's side).

One of Steve's most prized possessions was a blanket Marig had made for him using his race t-shirts. He had a very special relationship with Marig. From 1983 through 1986, they had lived across the hall from each other in Steve's parents' house. After Steve and I bought a house in 1987, he continued to visit his grandmother on a weekly basis. Eventually, Steve wrote Marig's unpublished story about how she survived the Armenian massacre.

Naps, 1987

Steve loved to take naps. He could fall asleep anywhere and reveled in it. In 1981, Steve took me to meet his grandmother Nana (his Mom's Mom) in Brooklyn. Due to our age difference, I was worried how the family would perceive our relationship. Nana made us her famous meatballs and manicotti. After lunch, we sat down to chat. Within five minutes, Steve was sound asleep and it was just Nana and I struggling to find conversation. Steve and I would always laugh at that memory.

In 1999, Steve took me to see the Broadway play *Fosse* and got us front row seats. During the "Hey Big Spender" number, one of the singers leans over the bar at the edge of the stage and sings directly to Steve. I turn to look at Steve and his head is back, slack jaw and sound asleep, completely oblivious to the singing and the sound of the orchestra.

Steve napping in Sanibel Island in 1987, probably after the "exhausting" recreational tandem bike ride we took.

Naps, 2010

During more than one Ironman event, Steve enjoyed a quick, mid-race nap. At Lake Placid, Steve had found a beautiful spot just off part of the run course. Depending how he felt during the run, he would go off course to his nap spot, lay down by the brook, and take a quick nap. As part of the Ironman training camp he conducted each year, athletes toured a camp highlight: Steve's nap spot! As it always was with Steve, "The Beauty is in the Balance"; only Steve would stop to take a nap while racing an Ironman event. Steve was the most unique, interesting, intelligent, and fun person I have ever known in my life.

Steve pointing out his Ironman Lake Placid nap spot to his 2010 training camp participants.

Steve's actual Ironman Lake Placid nap site.

Grand Turk, 1988

Our Grand Turk visit turned out to be the vacation from hell. I convinced Steve that we had to go because I had heard the scuba diving was off the charts. The airline lost our luggage, and the first hotel room we had was dirty and dusty. After complaining to management, they changed our room. The hotel was near a prison and protesters were riding around in jeeps with bullhorns inciting people to revolt. We tried to make the best of it and continued our vacation. We rented a scooter and it died somewhere in the middle of the island. A hotel-organized "island excursion" consisted of sitting in the back of a pickup truck where we were taken to the driver's brother-in-law's house. At his house, there was a tiny bar with a disco ball over it. Another night, we walked to a restaurant and a sleazy character gives me a suggestive handshake. When we left the restaurant, Steve took a knife to protect me just in case the guy was still around. Steve and I quickly went back to the hotel and barricaded the door. As we laid in bed, we worried the ceiling fan was going to fall down and chop our heads off in the middle of the night. Steve wanted to leave early, but I thought the diving was too good to leave, so we stayed to do one more dive. As we waited on the beach for the dive boat to pick us up, we watched as it crashed into a reef. We met a local guy who offered to take us diving. He was stoned most of the time and lived in a termite-ridden shack, but we were grateful for his services as he took us on the best dives we ever had.

Island excursion.

Restaurant where we stole a knife for the walk home.

Thanks Sweetie,
I will alaveys treasure my memory of watching you play with the cowfish, it was worth every penny.
Love always Steve

   While I was looking for the photos of this trip, the above note Steve had written to me after the trip popped out. (A cowfish is an interesting fish that we enjoyed seeing in tropical water dives.) In spite of that note, he never did let me choose our vacation spots after that.

The German Connection, 1990s – 2000s

Annette first met Steve when he came to her training pool in Darmstadt, Germany, to conduct a swim clinic. She was only seventeen, but Steve was impressed with her swim technique and asked if she could be the assistant coach and translate the swimming part. Over the years, Annette continued to work closely with Steve at various swimming, cycling, and triathlon camps and clinics in the U.S. and Europe.

To quote from Annette's email to me after Steve passed; "We had a great time, Steve and I, and I learned a lot from him—especially his way of believing in a person. He told me I could have a triathlon event in Frankfurt. When he first told me I thought he is (how do you say) over his mind? Finally, seven years later I did start the Frankfurt City Triathlon. Steve always saw that opportunity."

From the first moment, Annette liked Steve. After the clinic, they went to dinner and Annette asked Steve, "What is your job?" She told me she will never forget his answer. Steve replied, "Oh, I just send out some e-mails and do some coaching." At this time, Annette was finishing school and starting to go to college and she thought to herself, "This sounds great and I would love to do that." Later on she realized that Steve is doing a lot more than a two-hour per day job.

As Annette reminisces, "So Steve made me

Steve and his good friend, and German business partner, Annette.

want to create my way of life just like his. Coaching, and I love it still, every lesson, every person I work with. So much Steve gave to me I give to my team as well. Steve had a big picture in his mind. He told me, 'You can have your own company, you can have an event in Frankfurt, we can have clinics in Mallorca or anywhere.' And he was right. I just love my life and my job. He was the only one just living the same life I do."

One final word from Annette: "My first race with Steve was the Mighty Hamptons with the German timing team. After all the work, we had a great BBQ Dinner at the beach. One of the timers could not stop saying how great it was and Steve just answered, 'Welcome to my life.' We had so much fun and it was a fantastic night. I still love to remember it."

Team Total Training (TTT), 1990s – 2015

*This is the TTT logo. Steve started TTT in the 1990s
with just a few close friends. The team grew over the
years due to Steve's great reputation in the triathlon
world and his coaching style.*

In an email on January 26, 2014, Steve had the following to say to members of TTT:

What's in a triathlon team? Interesting question to ponder. Triathlon is an individual sport. So is swimming or cross country running. But in those sports, there are more opportunities for 'team' competition such as swim or track meets. Yes, there is the USAT club championships, but that event is a small part of the sport of triathlon. So back to the question of what's in a triathlon team and, more specifically, what is our team, TTT?

I could tell you the who we are and what we do……. who cares about that, every club/team has that; been around since 1998, athletes of all ages and sports not just triathlon.. many use one or two of tri sports for other goals; camaraderie, nice parties (great parties), cool uniforms, all levels beginners to Hawaii Ironman, age group champs; blah blah blah. What I want to talk about is the WHY. Why does TTT exist and why would any of us want to be a part of its culture?

It is a spirit that TTT offers. You can't hold it, you can't bottle it, and you can't fake it. A collective energy of a group of people connected through sport in a way to support each other, even those not met personally. Whether it is a teammate doing her first pool triathlon, or a veteran doing his umpteenth long distance tri, they have a little boost being a part of our community. For the most part, we drop our egos and give each workout and race our best effort—knowing the race is almost always within. TTT has only one rule: Have fun. Alright, maybe two rules—be kind to animals. You can race or not, train or not, share or not. Be authentic, be who you are. Many have said, when you see another TTT athlete on the course or out training with their TTT gear and get a wave, it's pretty cool. TTT is in the heart.

TTT is that indomitable spirit in all of us that says, yeah, I can do this and you can too, let's give it a go and have fun on the way! TTT: "The Beauty is in the Balance."

Steve cheering teammates on the Ocean to Sound Relay Run, year unknown.

Steve loved training and racing with team members. When he wasn't training or racing, he was cheering his team on. Steve was very passionate about TTT.

One of Steve's favorite things to do was to customize an award for each team member that attended the annual team party. That could be up to one hundred or more awards each party! He would create the name of the award that was unique to the individual for that year. It could have been "Most Improved Open Water Swimmer," for example, or "Live to Tell" (my award one year when I found my way back to the hotel in Mallorca on my bike in a raging storm). Steve would then present the award to the teammate at the party and give a short speech to explain why that person received the award. This part of the party could get pretty long, but everyone was patient as they knew they would have their turn to shine with Steve. Steve had a knack for making people feel they were the most important person in the world when he was talking to them. Team members have treasured and saved these awards for many years.

TTT athlete Stan Lawrence benefited from Steve's commitment and his reward system. "Steve was incredibly passionate about the sport of triathlon and its associated healthy lifestyle. I will always have fond memories of training and trying to become a better swimmer with Steve's coaching. He was a fabulous person and thoughtful gentleman. I proudly display the team trophy Steve gave me at one of the year-end parties. The award was for Honorable Body Art. Steve often commented on a tattoo I have depicting the POW/MIA symbol and associated barbwire symbolizing captivity. He was very grateful to see veterans honor veterans. I will never forget that simple but heartfelt gesture. I am honored to say I was a friend and a teammate. God Bless Steve!"

Natalie Penny, TTT head coach, was also grateful for Steve's passion. "Steve gave so much love and hope to many, and built a playground for us all to build, grow, and rebuild again. He took great joy from seeing us all blossom. He was a very public figure here on Long Island as well as abroad. As public as he was, Steve was also intensely private. We share the grief in loss of our coach, friend, boss, and brother, and I, personally, will be forever grateful to have been his athlete, his teammate, and his friend. As he did for so many, he taught me how be the best I can be, and shared the same with my children and in particular my son, Jeremy."

Stan Lawrence TTT award,
2010.

Natalie Penny TTT awards,
2005-2012.

Steve would love to participate in triathlons with the athletes on his team. In one race, Steve and two of his favorite female athletes (Natalie Penny being one of them) all finished within eleven seconds of each other. The fact that athletes he coached could come so close to his times and even beat him in a race was more than he could ever ask for—humble and unassuming Steve thrived on the successes of his students.

TTT at Heekscher Park, 2008; Photo Credit: TOM RUDD Photography.

Steve with two teammates at Ironman Lake Placid expo, 2005.

TTT at Ironclad Triathlon, 2009.

Youth in Sport, 2000s

Steve was a pioneer in introducing the sport of triathlon to children. Since the 1990s, Steve had created youth events to introduce children to multi-sport in an environment where they felt like a winner, regardless of when they crossed the finish line. There were no trophies awarded; the rewards were having fun and the enjoyment of participation. In addition, Steve created a junior tri team (TTT Juniors). It was open to anyone who wanted to be a part of it, regardless of ability. Many of the junior members were children of the adult team members and Steve structured it so that the family could all go to swim practice together, with the juniors having their own dedicated coaches and swim lanes. Steve was a great role model for these children and many of these juniors are now accomplished young adults.

Two Team Total Training Junior team members with Steve at one of his company's youth events.

Steve the "Pied Piper" at one of his company's youth events.

Mallorca, Spain, 2000s

There are so many great stories of the cycling camps Steve held annually in Mallorca for many years. At the top of San Salvador mountain, there was a cafe where we would warm our chilled bones and regroup for the long bike journey back to the hotel. Steve would always lead the athletes back to the resort. Steve's top priority in these camps was the safety of the riders and he always got everyone back safely.

I believe it was in 2005, there were several groups of us climbing San Salvador. Of course, Steve's group was near the top and I was in the slow caboose group. As I climbed on the switchbacks, I heard one of the athletes singing, "I'm all out of gears..." to the melody of the Air Supply song "All out of Love." Sound has a strange way of traveling in the mountains and I heard it very clearly. I think that has been the only time I have ever laughed while climbing a mountain on a bike.

On another trip, one of the cyclists in our group had stopped at a midway point on Cap Formentor—at the same location where tour buses would stop for the views. A couple of German tourists were very excited because they thought he was Lance Armstrong.

Cyclists at top of San Salvador, 2007.

Each night after our rides, we would all share our stories at dinner with Steve as the emcee. It was Mallorca, where we all learned the German saying for wedgie: "Arsch frißt Hose." It is loosely translated to "my ass is eating my pants."

At each nightly dinner, Steve awarded someone the "No Whining" button by popular vote. Whoever complained the most on that day's ride would have to wear the button on the following day's ride. Over time, the "No Whining" button was awarded to the person who had every right to whine on that day's ride, but always remained cheerful and non complaining. Leave it to Steve and his positive influence on the group to turn something negative into a positive.

Ride back to resort, 2007; May the
wind be always at your back, Steve.

Vacations, 1982 – 2000

Steve and I were very lucky to have traveled to many beautiful places in this country and abroad. There was a period of time where Steve traveled a lot for business. If I couldn't go with him, he would make it a point to check out the scene to see if it was a place he thought we might like to return to together; we often did return at his recommendation, and he was always spot on!

Now, I like to think that Steve is scoping out heaven for me.

Cheeca Lodge in the Florida Keys, 1982.

Steve and I always laughed at the memories of this vacation. We were in no financial position to be eating at a restaurant at the high end Cheeca Lodge in the Florida Keys. We were so out of our league that we were afraid to ask for a second piece of bread.

Newport, Rhode Island at a lifeguard tournament, 1987.

St. Croix where Steve competed in a triathlon, 1989.

Red Rocks, Colorado, 1991.

Del Mar, California, 1992.

IBM Golden Circle in Orlando, FL,
1994.

Tucson hike, 1996.

We were staying at a B&B and decided to go hiking in the desert nearby before breakfast. Well, we got lost and ran out of water, but we were more upset over missing our pancake breakfast. Thankfully, we eventually found our way back to the B&B and they had held breakfast for us.

Swimming with the dolphins
in Bermuda, 1998.

I never knew my Dad's dad. I had been told there was a town in Italy near Turin called Entraque, where half of the town had Mellano as a last name. Steve took me there to help me find my roots. Although I never did find my father's family origins, visiting this tiny town in northwest Italy was such a wonderful memory for us. As with any of my great adventures with Steve, food was involved.

On our way to Entraque, Steve told me the food at the Italian truck stops was amazing. At the sound of "truck stop," I imagined fast food restaurants. But as always, Steve was on target—especially when it came to food. On our journey, we stopped at a truck stop on the autostrada (highway). The chef was preparing a delicious pasta dish with freshly grated Parmesan cheese, and the tiramisu was just made. We paid for our pasta and dessert and headed to a table. When it came time to have our tiramisu, Steve started wandering around to see where we could get coffee to have with dessert. A nice Italian man who spoke very little English asked Steve if he could help him. The man understood what Steve was looking for and said, "Ah, yes, Americans." He explained that in Italy, you ate the dessert first, then had your coffee. This was the reason the coffee bar was on the other side of the food area. So Steve and I did as the Italians do in Italy; we ate our tiramisu, then had our coffee.

Entraque, Italy, 1999.

Paris for my birthday, 2000.

Cycling, 1987 - 2008

My first time on a road-bike tandem (vs. a leisure, fun tandem) was in the early nineties in Colorado Springs. It was my first road-bike ride, tandem or not! We rented the bike and it took us twenty minutes to start the ride because I was petrified to clip in. Steve was extremely patient with me. He had such patience with all beginners, including me.

Later in the nineties, Steve took me on a road-bike tandem ride up to Palomar Mountain in California. I had no idea how hard it must have been for him to lug me up the mountain, pulling my weight, until I started road biking myself years later. Steve mistakenly took a wrong turn before the journey up Palomar. All of a sudden, he made a quick u-turn in the middle of the road and said, "Start pedaling fast." Since I was sitting behind him, I couldn't see what was going on, so I started asking questions. He said, "Just shut up and pedal." It didn't take long for me to realize we were racing away from a pack of snarling dogs that had been charging towards us—and they weren't looking for a pat on the head! I heard the barking and started pedaling as fast as I could, and because of Steve's power, we were able to get away and continue our journey up the mountain. The descent was frightening as we reached speeds up to 40MPH. We had to pull over a few times for my own sanity. At my request, Steve slowed us down, but it caused the brakes to start burning out the tires. Throughout this adventure, Steve maintained his patience with me and my anxieties.

Recreational tandem ride in the pouring rain, Sanibel Island, 1987.

Still smiling after our ride, 1987.

Steve and I at his Lake Placid triathlon camp, 2008.

Since I was so immersed in Steve's athletic world, I wanted more and more to become a participant vs. a spectator. I started road-biking later in life and I became one of those "all the gear and no idea" cyclists. My first bike was a hybrid with road-bike tires, lightweight frame and mountain bike style handlebars. I was petrified of falling, especially on down hills and riding with the typical road-bike handlebars (vs. mountain bike handlebars). Whenever I whined that I wanted to get a real road-bike, Steve always cautioned me by saying there are two kinds of bikers: those that have crashed, and those that will crash. He told me that I have to accept the fact that I will eventually crash.

When I came home one day and told him I bought a road-bike, he collapsed on the floor and said, "This is my worst nightmare." He knew I would struggle with controlling a road-bike because of my issues and fears. To quote a friend of ours, I've "got more issues than Sports Illustrated." Needless to say, I have had a few crashes over the years, though nothing serious. I always treasured the rides Steve completed with me. I know it was tortuous for him since I was so slow, but it was special for us. As motivation to finish the ride, food was always a part of our great adventures. Without fail, there was a meal stop scheduled at the end of each ride.

Cancer Survivor, 2007

This was the year Steve discovered my tonsil cancer. I was sitting across the table from him in our kitchen and I had let out a huge belly laugh in response to something hilarious he had said. Then Steve asked "What's that thing in your throat?" After that, he was by my side with his never-ending support, love, and devotion.

At one very low point during treatment, I was whining about my pain and Steve said, "Do you want me to get the hats?" I asked, "What hats?" Steve replied, "Hats for the pity party." We both laughed so hard. From that moment on, I knew I would survive cancer.

Maui Xterra triathlon championship, 2007. Steve, so happy the finish line was in sight and I was cancer free.

Our "pity party" hats.

Lake Placid Ironman, 2005 – 2012

Steve was so passionate about everything he did in life. Team Total Training and Lake Placid Ironman were no exceptions. The story was not that Steve finished the race fourteen times since its inception in 1999; the more important stories involved the coaching and training he did for the team's athletes. Steve coached the person, not just the athlete. Every year, Steve would gather the team athletes for a group photo the day before the event and gave them each a personalized handwritten note of encouragement. Steve was not just a fountain of knowledge about this event for the athletes; he was also a great source of emotional support for them—whether it was their first Ironman or their tenth.

Steve always had a great way of providing a teaching moment to all the people that his life touched. I remember one of the teammates, Mike, was doing his first Ironman in 2006. Like most athletes, Mike had many questions for Steve. If you knew Mike, you can appreciate that he had ten times as many questions as anyone else. The day before the race, Mike was inundating Steve with questions (keep in mind, there may have been ten to fifteen other teammates asking Steve questions, plus he was preparing for his own race). Steve told Mike, with great humor and kindness, that he gets one question an hour. Mike came back two hours later with two questions and Steve said, "Sorry, Mike. If you don't use your question in the hour, it expires and they don't roll over." Of course, Steve did answer the two questions and many more after that.

I was just a spectator, but Steve grabbed my hand so I could soak in the glory of the finish line with him. Steve always said the spectators had a tougher day than the athletes since no one was handing the spectators food and sunscreen, nor did they get a massage at the end of the race.

Steve and I crossing the finish line at Ironman Lake Placid, 2005.

Team Total Training (TTT) athletes at
Lake Placid Ironman, 2007.

After Steve passed away, Vic Rivas (TTT athlete on far right of photo) said in an email to me:

Coach, you touched and improved our lives in so many ways. Ten years ago, I was going through a divorce and not knowing where my life would take me next. My brother then introduced myself to you and the team. Immediately I began experiencing some of the greatest times in my life. I'll always be grateful for all of the time we spent together. From swimming in the pool, to the Bear Mountain trips, Mad Man Wednesdays, Cedar Creek, Tobay Open water swims, the camps, and of course the races. But more importantly your friendship and the time we spent together on and off the course. You were able to bring out so much more in myself as an athlete while teaching me some very important life lessons. Somehow, when we all got together, whatever stress we had was almost instantly forgotten. You were always an important part in my life and always will be. R.I.P. Coach, I love you.

TTT athlete Deb Savarese says, "You've changed my life forever. There's no way to repay that. All I can do is pay it forward as best I can—which still will never be enough."

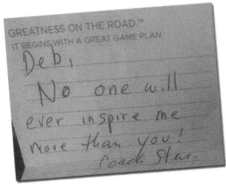

Steve's note to Deb prior to her first Ironman in 2010.

Steve and Deb, Lake Placid Ironman in 2010.

Sean McCarthy, a TTT athlete, sent this to me: "My fondest memory of Steve and Ironman had to be in 2012. I was coming down Mirror Lake Drive in Lake Placid on my second and final run loop, about to enter the oval, and Steve was about to start his second run loop. He somehow knew that I was coming down the hill and was standing there waiting for me. The flood gates opened before I even got close to him. We hugged, he congratulated me on my performance, and I cried all the way to the finish line. I will never forget that moment and I get teary eyed every time I think about it."

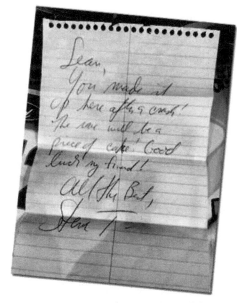

Steve's note to Sean prior to his Ironman, 2012.

Wataru was one of the early TTT team members; he also worked at many of the events for Steve's company. I remember he introduced himself as "Walter," but Steve thought for sure he must have had a Japanese first name and asked him. Walter replied that he tells everyone his name is Walter because it is easier for people to say and spell. Steve thought Walter should be called by his true name if that was what he really wanted. To this day, to all his team friends, Walter is called by his given Japanese name, Wataru. Steve had an instinctive nature to care about the smallest details.

Steve and Wataru at Lake Placid
Ironman finish line, 2011.

Bunnies, 2010

In 2006, Steve was conducting a "brick," or bike/run workout, in a local park for his triathlon team (it is called brick because that is how your legs feel when you are done.). The park has a one-mile loop where we would bike multiple laps. We started to notice a bunch of rabbits living in the park. One that caught our eye was a heli-lop (one ear up, one ear down) with black and white colorings like Charlie Brown's dog, so we named him Snoopy. Steve and I soon realized these were domestic rabbits, probably dumped by someone who could no longer take care of them. We felt these rabbits would not survive the winter so we contacted Long Island Rabbit Rescue (LIRRG) to see if they would take these rabbits. As with many rescue organizations, LIRRG is not a shelter and had no place to house these rabbits. They did offer to assist in capturing and providing supplies and education if we could foster or adopt one or more of the rabbits, but there were no guarantees they could capture any of them—including Snoopy.

Since Steve and I felt we were too busy for a pet, Steve sent an email to the triathlon team asking if anyone could foster or adopt a rabbit. A few people said yes, so we gave LIRRG the go-ahead to attempt to rescue Snoopy! The potential offers to foster or adopt Snoopy fell through, so Steve and I became rabbit owners. In 2010, a LIRRG volunteer asked if we could foster a baby bunny she found fending for himself in the woods. Steve and I took him in and kept him in a cage in the living room so it would appear to be a temporary situation. My cousin's husband, Allan, came by one day and saw the rabbit in the living room. We told him we were fostering. He asked us if we gave the rabbit a name and Steve and I said, "Yes, Budgie." Allan immediately said, "You are keeping him," and he was so right! That was five years ago and Steve and I were officially "failed fosterers." As someone once told us, there are worse things in life to fail at.

Steve and Snoopy.

Steve and Budgie.

Butterfly Kisses, 1982 and 2012

New Jersey quarry, 1982.

Whenever the opportunity presented itself, whether in a pool or open water, Steve would come out of the water for air during the butterfly stroke and blow me a kiss. He knew I loved that.

Ironman Lake Placid, 2012.

This was the last year Steve did Ironman Lake Placid. Every year when he came out of the swim and up the ramp to bike transition, he would always look for me in one spot so he could give me a kiss. This is after a 2.4 mile swim, before he headed out on a 112 mile bike, and then a 26.2 mile run. He was an Ironman not just in sport but in life.

Hawaii, 1990s – 2000s

*Steve and I and the "rescued" ones at Waimea Canyon
in Kauai, 1995.*

Rip is a long-time friend of Steve's. Steve and I "rescued" Rip and two of Rip's friends in 1995 at the start of the Kalalau Trail in Kauai. Kalalau Trail can be quite treacherous, especially in the rain; it is slippery and there is nothing stopping you from falling down the side of the cliff. Steve and I were going to do the easy hike early that morning. At the entrance to the trail, we saw Rip and his friends washing the mud off their bodies at the outside shower at the start of the trail. I never saw three men so happy to see us, especially when Steve asked them if they wanted to go to our rental condo to take a hot shower. It turns out they had started hiking the day before, later in the afternoon, and by the time they turned around, it was getting dark. It took them hours in the dark of climbing back down by the light of an Ironman watch.

Another great Rip memory Steve and I cherished is when we spent a night at Rip's dad's farm in upstate New York one year. Rip's family promotes plant-based diets and we had the most delicious vegan meals during our stay there. On our return trip down the New York State Thruway, Steve took the first exit in search of a diner where we had coffee and greasy bacon and egg sandwiches. As Steve would always say, "The Beauty is in the Balance."

*Steve and Rip at the XTERRA Maui
Championships, 2003.*

We called this location Contemplation Rock, which was near Annini beach. We used to watch our flower lei's drift away in the surf and give thanks for the blessed life we were living.

Kauai, 1997.

Maui XTERRA championships finish line, 2004.

Kalalau trail hike, 2008
We hiked this trail every year we returned to Kauai.

Maui XTERRA championships awards dinner, 2008.

In October of 2010, Steve wrote about his thoughts on retirement. In anticipation of retiring together in the near future, we bought ourselves retirement watches in Maui.

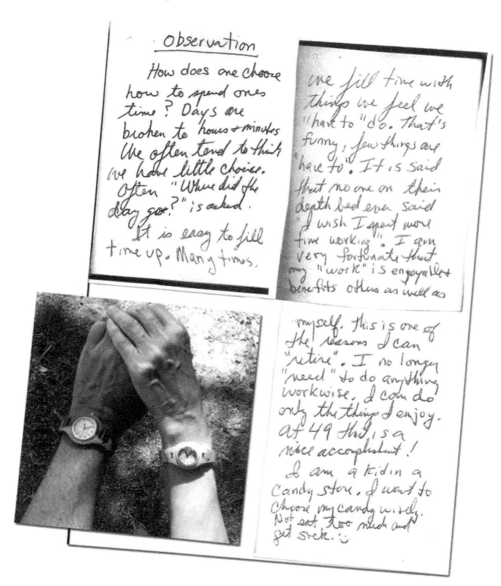

Observation

How does one choose how to spend ones time? Days are broken to hours & minutes. We often tend to think we have little choices. Often "Where did the day go?" is asked.

It is easy to fill time up. Many times, we fill time with things we feel we "have to" do. That's funny, few things are "have to". It is said that no one on their death bed ever said "I wish I spent more time working". I am very fortunate that my "work" is enjoyable & benefits others as well as myself. This is one of the reasons I can "retire". I no longer "need" to do anything workwise. I can do only the things I enjoy. At 49 this is a nice accomplishment!

I am a kid in a candy store. I want to choose my candy wisely. Not eat too much and get sick. :)

Maui, 2011.

We are in our costume for the XTERRA Halloween Party—a pair of Thai pants. As it turned out, we couldn't walk very far in this outfit, so we opted out of going to the party and decided to stay in and just chill. I think Steve fell asleep within ten minutes of this photo; after all, he had done almost a five-hour grueling race that day. I cut him some slack on this one.

Every year when we went to Kauai, Steve and I would always seek out a hammock big enough to hold both of us. On this particular hammock at the Princeville hotel in Kauai, we both climbed into it and immediately rolled out. Lying in the sand, we felt we had never laughed so hard in our lives. They were true belly laughs that we were privileged to share many times in our lives together. I think these shared belly laughs are one of the things I will miss the most about Steve.

Kauai, 2011.

October 2012 was Steve's last time at the Maui XTERRA Championships. He had finished every one of the Championship races annually since 1996. Leaning against the tree is Steve's new mountain bike. :-) Every year that we went to Maui for this race, he said he was going to buy a new high-tech mountain bike. However, he always brought back his old faithful bike that stood out as an antique among the high-tech bikes of all the pros and elite-level athletes that were in the event.

Steve's mountain bike "training" in preparation for this event each year usually started in September in New York. This "training" consisted of cycling with me and going "off road" on the grass, or up and down the curb a few times. Steve loved doing this event for the challenge and the pure joy and beauty of it and was content to just finish it. It was not important to Steve to place in his age group.

One year, Steve decided to *intensify* his "training" while we were in Kauai on vacation the week before XTERRA. He declined to go on a scuba dive with me one day as he said he needed to "train" off road for XTERRA. I think the real reason he didn't dive with me was because he was afraid he would be attacked by a shark. As Steve got older, his fear of shark attacks grew, especially since Hawaii is known for having a shark population. As it turns out, I dove with no shark attacks and Steve got bitten on the calf by a dog while he was riding.

Steve with his new "mountain bike" leaning against the tree, 2012.

EPILOGUE

*"T'is better to have loved and lost
than never to have loved at all"*
–Alfred Lord Tennyson

My labor of love and my tribute to Steve has come to an end. It has only scratched the surface of his life. With all the love, caring, and time Steve gave of himself to others, I never felt cheated. He gave so much of himself to me as well. There are many stories I have not shared, and many more I have forgotten. But my hope is that, after reading this book, you can walk away with some piece of Steve's goodness that I have attempted to articulate. Perhaps with what you may have gleaned from this book will help you make a worthwhile change in your own life. Steve's ability to positively impact people's lives during life and in death will be Steve's true legacy.

The French have several ways to say goodbye. Two come to mind: "au revoir," which means until we meet again; and "adieu" which has a sense of finality. Since we will see each other again, I bid my Stevie au revoir...

"I think the saddest people always try their hardest to make people happy because they know what it's like to feel absolutely worthless and they don't want anyone else to feel like that."
—Robin Williams

CPSIA information can be obtained
at www.ICGtesting.com
Printed in the USA
BVOW10s1507130616

451837BV00008B/15/P